Arctic Sea Ice Decline: Projected Changes in Timing and Extent of Sea Ice in the Bering and Chukchi Seas

By D.C. Douglas

Open-File Report 2010–1176

U.S. Department of the Interior
U.S. Geological Survey

U.S. Department of the Interior
KEN SALAZAR, Secretary

U.S. Geological Survey
Marcia K. McNutt, Director

U.S. Geological Survey, Reston, Virginia: 2010

For more information on the USGS—the Federal source for science about the Earth,
its natural and living resources, natural hazards, and the environment,
visit *http://www.usgs.gov* or call 1–888–ASK–USGS.

For an overview of USGS information products, including maps, imagery, and publications,
visit *http://www.usgs.gov/pubprod*

To order this and other USGS information products, visit *http://store.usgs.gov*

Suggested citation:
Douglas, D.C., 2010, Arctic sea ice decline: Projected changes in timing and extent of sea ice in the Bering and
Chukchi Seas: U.S. Geological Survey Open-File Report 2010-1176, 32 p.

Contents

Figures

Tables

Conversion Factors

Multiply	By	To obtain
kilometer (km)	0.6214	mile (mi)
square kilometer (km^2)	0.3861	square mile (mi^2)

Temperature in degrees Celsius (°C) may be converted to degrees Fahrenheit (°F) as follows:
°F=(1.8×°C)+32.
Temperature in degrees Fahrenheit (°F) may be converted to degrees Celsius (°C) as follows:
°C=(°F-32)/1.8.

List of Acronyms

20C3M	GHG forcing scenario, 20th Century Experiment (simulation)
A1B	GHG forcing scenario, 'business as usual', 2100 CO_2 stabilizes ~715 ppm
A2	GHG forcing scenario, 2100 CO_2 increases to ~850 ppm
AR4	fourth and most recent IPCC reporting period
CCSM3	Community Climate System Model version 3
CMIP3	Coupled Model Intercomparison Project phase 3
CO_2	carbon dioxide
GCM	general circulation model
GHG	greenhouse gas
GMAT	global mean annual temperature
HadGEM1	Hadley Centre Global Environmental Model version 1
IPCC	Intergovernmental Panel on Climate Change
NSIDC	National Snow and Ice Data Center
SD1	multimodel GCM subset based on 1 standard deviation tolerance
SD2	multimodel GCM subset based on 2 standard deviation tolerance
SRES	Special Report on Emission Scenarios
USGS	U.S. Geological Survey
ppm	parts per million

Arctic Sea Ice Decline: Projected Changes in Timing and Extent of Sea Ice in the Bering and Chukchi Seas

By D.C. Douglas

Abstract

The Arctic region is warming faster than most regions of the world due in part to increasing greenhouse gases and positive feedbacks associated with the loss of snow and ice cover. One consequence has been a rapid decline in Arctic sea ice over the past 3 decades—a decline that is projected to continue by state-of-the-art models. Many stakeholders are therefore interested in how global warming may change the timing and extent of sea ice Arctic-wide, and for specific regions. To inform the public and decision makers of anticipated environmental changes, scientists are striving to better understand how sea ice influences ecosystem structure, local weather, and global climate. Here, projected changes in the Bering and Chukchi Seas are examined because sea ice influences the presence of, or accessibility to, a variety of local resources of commercial and cultural value. In this study, 21st century sea ice conditions in the Bering and Chukchi Seas are based on projections by 18 general circulation models (GCMs) prepared for the fourth reporting period by the Intergovernmental Panel on Climate Change (IPCC) in 2007. Sea ice projections are analyzed for each of two IPCC greenhouse gas forcing scenarios: the A1B 'business as usual' scenario and the A2 scenario that is somewhat more aggressive in its CO_2 emissions during the second half of the century. A large spread of uncertainty among projections by all 18 models was constrained by creating model subsets that excluded GCMs that poorly simulated the 1979–2008 satellite record of ice extent and seasonality.

At the end of the 21st century (2090–2099), median sea ice projections among all combinations of model ensemble and forcing scenario were qualitatively similar. June is projected to experience the least amount of sea ice loss among all months. For the Chukchi Sea, projections show extensive ice melt during July and ice-free conditions during August, September, and October by the end of the century, with high agreement among models. High agreement also accompanies projections that the Chukchi Sea will be completely ice covered during February, March, and April at the end of the century. Large uncertainties, however, are associated with the timing and amount of partial ice cover during the intervening periods of melt and freeze. For the Bering Sea, median March ice extent is projected to be about 25 percent less than the 1979–1988 average by mid-century and 60 percent less by the end of the century. The ice-free season in the Bering Sea is projected to increase from its contemporary average of 5.5 months to a median of about 8.5 months by the end of the century. A 3-month longer ice-free season in the Bering Sea is attained by a 1-month advance in melt and a 2-month delay in freeze, meaning the ice edge typically will pass through the Bering Strait in May and January at the end of the century rather than June and November as presently observed.

Introduction

Sea ice plays an important role in the Arctic climate system by modulating the exchange of heat between a warm ocean and a cold atmosphere (Barry and others, 1993). How global warming may change the contemporary status of sea ice raises both economic and cultural concerns. Short-term ice anomalies can influence novel weather patterns even at temperate latitudes (Budikova, 2009), although long-term changes can alter the structure of marine ecosystems (Grebmeier and others, 2006, 2010). In a future with less sea ice, commercial and subsistence fisheries in the Arctic will contend with changes in species composition and productivity (Vilhjálmsson and Hoel, 2005). Marine shipping and commercial resource extraction will realize new opportunities but introduce new environmental stresses (Nordquist and others, 2010). Less sea ice is expected to affect the distribution, abundance, and diversity of Arctic marine mammals (Moore and Huntington, 2008); many of which are important to the cultural heritage and subsistence lifestyle of coastal native communities throughout the circumpolar north (Hovelsrud and others, 2008).

During the past 3 decades, satellite data indicate increasing temperatures and decreasing sea ice throughout the Arctic (Comiso and others, 2003; Johannessen and others, 2004; Arctic Climate Impact Assessment, 2005; Meier and others, 2007; Serreze and others, 2007; Perovich and Richter-Menge, 2009). During 1979–2009, September ice extent Arctic-wide decreased at an average linear rate of 79,000 km^2/yr (National Snow and Ice Data Center, 2010), an area roughly the size of Nebraska. During the recent decade, however, the trend in Arctic sea ice loss has accelerated (Comiso and others, 2008). Arctic-wide, seven of the lowest annual minimum ice extents since 1979 have occurred in the past 8 years (2002–2009). The record minimum extent in September 2007 (4.3 million km^2) was 42 percent less than the 1979–1988 average.

Observed trends of sea ice loss at regional scales exhibit a breadth of spatial and temporal variability (Meier and others, 2007). The most pronounced sea ice declines in the Arctic basin have been in the Barents and Chukchi Seas—the two regions that receive the largest inputs of ocean and air masses from southern latitudes. During 1979–2006, September ice extent in the Chukchi and Barents Seas decreased 26 and 22 percent per decade, respectively (Meier and others, 2007). In areas south of the Arctic basin, sea ice fluctuations are more directly influenced by natural variations in extratropical weather patterns. Winter ice extent in the Bering Sea has been particularly variable. March ice extent in the Bering Sea was near record minimum during 2000–2005, but near record maximum during 2007–2010.

The future status of sea ice in the Bering and Chukchi Seas is a topic of particular interest in the two bordering countries, the United States (Alaska) and Russia (Chukotka Autonomous Region). The Bering Sea supports one of the most productive fisheries in the world (Bering Ecosystem Study, 2004) and the eastern Chukchi Sea has large petroleum reserves that are currently being explored and leased (Minerals Management Service, 2008). Both seas support a high diversity and abundance of resident and migratory marine mammals and birds (Springer and others, 1999). Because sea ice influences the presence of, or accessibility to, these varied resources, a broad spectrum of private and commercial stakeholders are interested in how global warming may change the timing and extent of sea ice in the Bering and Chukchi Seas.

The most sophisticated projections of future climate are based on general circulation models (GCMs). GCMs emulate the thermodynamic and dynamic transfers of energy and momentum, within and between the oceans, atmosphere, biosphere, geosphere, and cryosphere in a fully coupled global framework (McGuffie and Henderson-Sellers, 2005). Numerous GCMs have been developed by institutions worldwide. The GCM outputs are shared among all scientists through the World Climate Research Program's Coupled Model Intercomparison Project phase 3 (CMIP3) multi-model dataset (Meehl and others, 2007a). Under auspices of the United Nations Framework Convention on Climate Change, member nations of the Intergovernmental Panel on Climate Change (IPCC) review literature about the GCM projections and publish reports that evaluate the risk of climate change caused by human activities. The fourth and most recent series of IPCC reports (AR4) was published in 2007.

When forced with unmitigated scenarios of increasing atmospheric greenhouse gas (GHG) concentrations, all CMIP3 GCMs project declines in Arctic sea ice during the 21st century (Meehl and others, 2007b) but the magnitudes and rates of decline vary considerably among models (Zhang and Walsh, 2006). Under a similar forcing scenario, different GCMs project different outcomes due to natural climate variability and to structural and parameterization differences among the models (Knutti, 2008; Hawkins and Sutton, 2009). The spread of uncertainty among projections of a multi-model ensemble is thus a mixture of simulating the Earth's natural climate variability combined with inherent modeling uncertainty. The spread commonly is used as a benchmark for describing the uncertainty of climate model results, but it does not necessarily capture the full range of uncertainty that might otherwise be obtained if more model runs were conducted, or if new models were developed that incorporated more elements of the climate system.

Culling models that poorly simulate observational data, or deemphasizing their weight in a multi-model ensemble is a commonly applied approach to constrain the spread of modeling uncertainty (Wang and Overland, 2009; Boe and others, 2010). Subsetting GCMs aims at reducing the breadth of uncertainty among ensemble models and to purportedly improve the GCMs collective forecasting proficiencies. The basic premise underlying the concept of subsetting assumes that models that demonstrate better proficiency in simulating observations may be better models for projecting future conditions, but there is no guarantee that such models actually possess better long-term extrapolations (Gleckler and others, 2008). Given the wide range of raw model results, however, culling those models that grossly misrepresent observations is a reasonable step toward excluding less reliable projections.

Here, I present a comprehensive examination of 21st century sea ice projections in the Bering and Chukchi Seas by 18 CMIP3 GCMs. Although future sea ice conditions in the Bering and Chukchi Seas is a topic of broad interest, the primary impetus for this study was to provide an analysis of future habitat of the Pacific walrus (*Odobenus rosmarus divergens*), a pinniped species strongly associated with sea ice. The study area extends over the extensive and shallow (greater than −150 m) continental shelf waters of the Bering and Chukchi Seas (fig. 1). The northern and southern boundaries are terminated by steep shelf breaks, and the eastern and western boundaries are terminated by the contemporary range distribution of the Pacific walrus population (Fay, 1985). The Bering Sea and Chukchi Sea study areas encompass 934,000 and 709,000 km^2, respectively. The Chukchi Sea is one of seven commonly recognized shallow peripheral seas that surround the deep central Arctic Ocean. A prevailing northward flow of ocean currents through the Bering Strait strongly influences sea ice conditions in Chukchi Sea (Woodgate and others, 2010), as well as the thermal structure, nutrient loading, and freshwater budget of the Arctic Ocean (Woodgate and Aagaard, 2005). In the Bering Sea, the steep continental shelf-break promotes nutrient-rich upwellings that support a highly productive ecosystem (Springer and others, 1996), and limits the southernmost extent of winter ice formation (Alexander and Niebauer, 1981).

In this report, satellite observations of sea ice during the past 3 decades are presented to document current sea ice changes and to establish a baseline for comparing future changes. Projections and uncertainties are examined for the full 18-model ensemble and for two subsets that omit models that poorly simulate the satellite records of the extent and seasonality of ice cover. Results are presented for two unmitigated GHG forcing scenarios: A1B and A2 (Nakicenovic and others, 2000), with focus on the middle (2045–2054) and end (2090–2099) of the 21st century. In the A1B scenario, which is commonly called the 'business as usual' scenario, atmospheric CO_2 concentration roughly doubles and stabilizes at about 720 ppm by the end of the century. The A2 scenario is somewhat more aggressive than the A1B scenario after mid-century as CO_2 increases to about 850 ppm by 2100. Trends and uncertainties among the GCM sea ice projections are graphically illustrated and monthly maps are presented to convey a spatial context of the projected sea ice changes.

Methods

Modeled projections of sea ice concentration were obtained from the World Climate Research Programme's Coupled Model Intercomparison Project phase 3 (CMIP3) multi-model archive (Meehl and others, 2007a) for all GCMs that had monthly 21st century sea ice projections derived under each of two SRES greenhouse gas forcing scenarios (A1B and A2), as well as 20th century hindcasts from the 20C3M scenario. When the CMIP3 data were acquired in May 2009, a total of 18 GCMs met the criteria above (table 1). Data were obtained for one model run (run #1) of each GCM and forcing scenario. Salient features of the CMIP3 GCMs are summarized by Randall and others (2007, table 8.1). Satellite observations of monthly sea ice concentration were obtained from the National Snow and Ice Data Center (NSIDC) final data archives for 1979–2007 (Cavalieri and others, 1996) and from preliminary archives for 2008 (Meier and others, 2006). The GCM data were transformed and resampled (using the nearest neighbor distance protocol) to a 25-km-resolution polar stereographic grid that was congruent to the NSIDC grid of sea ice observations. Depending on a given GCMs spatial resolution and terrestrial representation, some coastal margins rendered missing ice concentration data after resampling to the 25-km grid.

For each month, and independently for the Bering Sea and Chukchi Sea study areas, the proportion of ice-covered ocean was calculated as the ratio of the summed area of pixels with equal to or greater than15 percent ice concentration to the summed area of all pixels with non-missing data. A ratio calculation was necessary to standardize the estimates of proportional ice cover because the GCMs varied in the total amount of the study area that was represented with non-missing ice concentration data. All area calculations accounted for distortions introduced by the polar stereographic map projection. A month was classified as ice-free for a given study area when the proportional ice cover was less than 10 percent. Attempts to use a smaller threshold for classifying an ice-free month tended to produce unstable results, owing in part to the coarse resolution of the raw GCM grids relative to the size of the study area, and to spurious estimates of summer ice along shorelines in the satellite observational data (Cavalieri and others, 1999).

Subsets of the 18 GCMs were independently constructed for each study area. Subsets were constructed based on criteria that evaluated a GCMs proficiency in simulating the observational record of sea ice over the past 3 decades. A GCM was included in a subset based on two criteria—one that considered the quantity of ice and another that considered its seasonality (Wang and Overland, 2009).

For the Bering Sea, models included in a subset were required to simulate the 1979–2008 mean ice extent in March to within 2 standard deviations of the observed mean. March is the month of maximum ice extent in the Bering Sea. For the Chukchi Sea, the same criteria were used but for September, the month of minimum ice extent. Seasonality of the ice was evaluated based on a model's proficiency in simulating the average number of ice-free months per year to within 2 standard deviations. Because ice-free months were uncommon in the Chukchi Sea until recently (even 1 standard deviation of the observed mean included zero), models included in a subset for the Chukchi Sea also were required to simulate at least 1 ice-free month during 1979–2008.

Henceforth, model subsets for the Bering and Chukchi Seas that were defined with a 2 standard deviation tolerance are referred to as "SD2" subsets. The same subsetting procedure described above was applied a second time to create a more restrictive subset for each study area based on a 1 standard deviation tolerance (henceforth termed the "SD1" subsets). By construct, SD1 is a subset of its SD2 counterpart.

The observational period was intentionally extended beyond the end of the 20th century to include recent years (2000–2008) of pronounced sea ice change in the Chukchi Sea. The GCM simulations from the 20th century experiment (20C3M) were extended to 2008 by populating the early years of the 21st century with ice projections from either the A1B or A2 scenarios. The entire model screening procedure described above was done twice, once using simulations that had been extended with the A1B scenario and once using simulations extended with the A2 scenario. Models selected in either of the two screenings were included in the final SD2 and SD1 subsets for each study area (table 1). The union of the two screenings was selected to increase the number of GCMs within a subset, but the net effect was modest in that 27 of the 31 total entries in table 1 were common to both screenings.

Ice observations and the projections by individual GCMs were averaged over 10-year (decadal) periods to integrate the Arctic's intrinsic interannual sea ice variability. For generalizing a multi-model ensemble, the median of the models' decadal averages is reported because the GCM ice projections were not assumed to be normally distributed. Decadal results typically are graphed with box and whisker notation (fig. 2) to provide information about the full range and distribution of the samples. Samples for the ice projections are the individual models of a respective GCM ensemble; hence the box and whisker plots convey information about the spread of model uncertainty within the ensemble.

Results

Sea Ice Observations

Because the Bering and Chukchi Seas are oriented strictly north and south of one another (fig. 1), summer ice retreat in the Chukchi Sea does not commence until the vast majority of ice in the Bering Sea has melted, and conversely, autumn ice formation in the Bering Sea begins after the Chukchi Sea has all but completely frozen. This unique seasonal dynamic is highlighted in figure 3, which plots monthly proportional ice cover in the Bering Sea with open water cover (the inverse of ice cover) in the Chukchi Sea. The spring and autumn transition months, defined here as the period when the ice edge is passing through the Bering Strait, are clearly evident in figure 3. Contemporary sea ice typically retreats northward through the Bering Strait in June and advances southward through the Strait in November.

Winter ice extent in the Bering Sea has shown little evidence of change during the past 30 years (fig. 3). During the most recent decade of satellite observations (1999–2008), monthly ice extents in the Bering Sea generally have been more variable (wider interquartile range) than the earliest decade (1979–1988), especially during months of rapid ice growth (December and January) and melt (May).

Summer ice cover in the Chukchi Sea has substantially declined (fig. 3). Presently, little ice remains at the end of the melt season in September. Ice-free conditions have been observed in September during several recent years, as well as August and October in 2005 and 2007. The Chukchi Sea freezes completely during the winter, a pattern that has not changed over the past 30 years. Because the transition months of June and November have remained unchanged, much larger areas of ice are presently melting and freezing in the Chukchi Sea over an equivalent time span.

GCM Subsets

Screening the GCMs substantially reduced the spread of uncertainty among models of the SD2 and SD1 subsets compared to that of the full 18-model ensemble—during the observational period (fig. 4). Ranges of uncertainty among the SD2 models typically were much less than the 18-model ensemble in all months. Similarly, the range of uncertainty among the SD1 subset typically was less than its SD2 counterpart.

Subsetting constrained the spread of uncertainty in all months in the Bering Sea. Median ice extents were more or less congruent among all three ensembles, indicating that screening excluded GCMs that simulated too little and too much ice. A slight positive bias in median ice extent during spring (April–May) was evident among all ensembles (fig. 4), indicating that the models tend to simulate a slightly later onset of the melt season compared to observations.

In the Chukchi Sea, the SD2 and SD1 model subsets simulated median sea ice observations more accurately than the 18-model ensemble, which substantially overestimated summer ice cover (fig. 4). Evidently, the Chukchi Sea subsets tended to exclude GCMs that simulated too much ice. Model subsets for the Chukchi Sea were less effective in reducing the spread of uncertainty compared to the Bering Sea model subsets, and were least effective constraining uncertainty during periods of melt and freeze.

Overall, the subsets aligned more closely with observations and contained less uncertainty compared to the 18-model ensemble, especially in March and September for the Bering and Chukchi Seas, respectively, by virtue of the methodology (fig. 4). Over the course of the century, the spread of uncertainty among model subsets also tended to be less than that of the full 18-model ensemble (fig. 5). Models that were extreme outliers during the observational period generally remained outliers when projected. This view is consistent with the assertion that subsetting renders a more defensible ensemble by excluding models that grossly misrepresent observations because biases tend to be persistent, while recognizing that the selected models do not necessarily guarantee accurate long-term projections.

21st Century Projections

Mid- and late-century median sea ice projections possessed a remarkable degree of within-decade congruency irrespective of the different model ensembles and GHG forcing scenarios (fig. 6). With few exceptions, median sea ice projections for the Bering and Chukchi Seas produce qualitatively similar projections regardless of the model ensemble (SD2, SD1, or all 18 models) or forcing scenario (A1B or A2). One subtle exception does occur at mid-century when the A2 scenario projects slightly more ice cover than the A1B scenario during several months (fig. 6). Although the A2 scenario commonly is regarded as more 'aggressive' because its atmospheric CO_2 concentrations are higher than the A1B scenario at the end of the century, the A1B scenario at mid-century has higher CO_2 and projects slightly warmer global temperature (Intergovernmental Panel on Climate Change, 2007) and slightly less sea ice arctic wide (Meehl and others, 2007b, fig. 10.13).

The congruency among projections from different model subsets and GHG scenarios (fig. 6) required simplifying the presentation of results hereafter, by focusing on just the A1B scenario because of its "business as usual" storyline and its prevalence in the literature, and in most cases, the SD2 subset because of its larger representation of GCMs.

Figure 7 is a simplified version of figure 6 that highlights the general patterns of projected sea ice change in the Bering and Chukchi Seas. Compared to the first decade of satellite observations, ice-free conditions are projected to develop in the Bering Sea about 1 month earlier by the end of the century. June is projected to experience the least amount of sea ice loss among all months. During July, extensive areas of ice melt in the Chukchi Sea as the shelf becomes ice free for 3 or more months. The spatial rate of ice formation in the autumn remains fairly constant, hence complete freeze of the Chukchi Sea is delayed about 1 month by mid-century and 2 months by late-century. Maximum ice extent in March in the Bering Sea at mid-century is projected to be 23 percent less than the first decade of satellite observations, and 58 percent less by late-century (table 2).

Figure 8 illustrates how subsetting affected the spread of model uncertainty in each month, similar to figure 3, but for projections at mid- and late-century rather than observations. In the Bering Sea, the subsets markedly reduced the spread in all months compared to the full 18-model ensemble. As might be expected, the spread of uncertainty among ice projections (fig. 8) was somewhat inflated compared to the observational period (fig. 4), but overall the subsetting was reasonably effective in culling the more extreme outliers of the full 18-model ensemble.

Among projections of future sea ice in the Chukchi Sea, however, subsetting was less effective in reducing the spread of uncertainty except during the mid-summer period of minimum ice cover (fig. 8). Although there is full agreement among the SD2 models that the Chukchi Sea will be ice free during August–October at the end of the century, uncertainty is prevalent during the spring and autumn months of extensive melt and freeze. The wide spread of uncertainty during the months of melt and freeze essentially reflects a disagreement among models in whether the ice-free season might last 3, 4, or possibly 5 months at the end of the century.

Although the median sea ice projections for the Chukchi Sea by the SD2 and SD1 model subsets were substantially different than the median projected by the18 model ensemble during the observational period (fig. 4), the difference diminishes by mid-century and disappears by late-century (fig. 8). That is, although several models were excluded from the Chukchi Sea subsets because the models simulated too much ice, by the end of the century, median sea ice projection by the SD2 and SD1 model subsets were essentially equivalent to the median projected by the 18-model ensemble.

Monthly maps of observed and projected median ice edges are presented in figure 9. Median decadal ice edges demarcate the boundary where greater than 50 percent of the individual maps in a given group had ice cover greater than15 percent concentration. Group sample size is 10 years for observed decades, and 10 years times the number of ensemble GCMs for future decades. Caution should be exercised not to over interpret local-scale details of the projected ice edges because an artificial degree of spatial resolution was introduced when the raw GCM data were converted to a 25-km grid.

Location of the ice edge during winter in the Bering Sea has remained relatively constant over the past 30 years (fig. 9). At mid-century, the ice edge is projected to be slightly north of its present location. At the end of the century, ice only begins to appear in the Bering Sea in January and the maximum winter extent in March is roughly one-half that of contemporary observations. Throughout the century, ice is projected to begin melting in the Bering Sea in April, with little if any ice remaining in May by late-century.

June has the least amount of projected ice change, as noted above and reiterated by the ice edge map in figure 9. Rapid melt thereafter largely frees the Chukchi Sea shelf of ice in August by mid-century, and in July by the end of the century. The ice does not substantively reappear over the Chukchi Sea shelf until November at mid-century, and not until December at the end of the century.

The qualitative characteristics of projected ice changes that are illustrated in the maps (fig. 9) are consistent with those that are plotted in figure 7. However, because of distinctly different methodological constructs, fractional changes in ice cover shown in figure 7 (that is, table 2) would not be precisely reproduced by calculating changes in the extent of area encompassed by the median ice edges.

The number of ice-free months per year for 5 decadal periods spanning the 21st century as projected by the 18 model ensemble and the SD2 and SD1 subsets are shown in figure 10. The ice-free season in the Bering Sea is projected to gradually increase from its present-day average of about 5.5 months to a median of about 8.5 months by the end of the century, an increase of 3 months overall but accompanied by considerable uncertainty among the individual models. Extending the ice-free period in the Bering Sea by 3 months stems from a 1-month advance in melt and a 2-month delay in freeze (fig. 7). In other words, the transition months of June and November, when the ice edge presently passes through the Bering Strait, are projected to shift to May and January by the end of the 21st century.

On average, the Chukchi Sea has been ice free for 1 month per year during the past decade (fig. 10). Subset medians project a 2-month ice-free season by mid-century and a 4-month ice-free season by the end of the century. Longer ice-free seasons in the Chukchi Sea are projected to be more or less balanced around September (fig. 7).

The number of years per decade that are projected to be ice free for each month in the Bering and Chukchi Seas is shown in figures 11 and 12. In contrast to figure 10, the values used to construct the monthly box and whisker plots in figures 11 and 12 are the number of ice-free years within a decade, rather than 10-year averages of total ice-free months within a year. Figures 11 and 12 convey details not only about the trajectories of change, but also about the behavior of model uncertainties through time.

In the Bering Sea, November has been ice free for 6 of the past 10 years (fig. 11). Most models project that by mid-century, the Bering Sea will be ice free in November every year, and all models project that November will be ice free by 2070–2079. The Bering Sea has never experienced ice-free conditions in December during the past decade. The median sea ice projections by the 18 model ensemble and the SD2 and SD1 subsets indicate that by mid-century the Bering Sea will be ice free in December for 3–5 years per decade, and that most years will be ice free later in the century but with higher uncertainty. January in the Bering Sea retains ice cover until late in the century, after which 3–6 years per decade are free of ice, again with considerable uncertainty among models. Nearly all models project that by mid-century, the Bering Sea will be persistently ice free in June, and most models project that May will begin to be intermittently ice free.

Most models project that by mid-century the Chukchi Sea will be ice free in September in most years, and that every year will be ice free in September by 2070–2079 (fig. 12). September's evolution of transitioning through a period of relatively high uncertainty among models into a period of high agreement recurs in August and October. In fact, the pattern underlies all months that transition toward ice-free conditions in both study areas (figs. 11 and 12). This signature pattern typifies a multi-model ensemble in which all models ultimately project the same outcome, but differ in the rate at which the outcome is achieved.

Discussion

Several studies have analyzed the CMIP3 GCM sea ice projections to investigate when the Arctic might first realize a summertime ice-free state under the 'business as usual' A1B forcing scenario. The studies have applied different methods to subset models or otherwise weight the full ensemble of models. Wang and Overland (2009) required models to simulate both mean ice extent and mean seasonality to within ±20 percent of observations, where seasonality was defined as the difference in ice extent between March and September. They concluded that the Arctic may become nearly ice free (< 1 million km^2) in September 2037, a result similar to that of Holland and others (2006) who estimated that the Arctic may become nearly ice free around 2040 based on projections by the CCSM3 model only. Zhang (2010) screened 43 model runs from 20 GCMs on their ability to emulate observed sea ice changes in response to increases in surface air temperature, and reported that the Arctic could become nearly ice free (< 1 million km^2) as early as the late 2030s (2037–2065). Rather than excluding models, Boe and others (2010) constrained a full ensemble of 18 GCMs by developing a regression of the projected mean percentage of sea ice remaining in September (during a 20-year period) as a function of the simulated September trend in 1979–2007. By examining the regression estimate and its confidence intervals at the point where they intercepted the observed trend, and iterating the analysis over an evolution of 20-year periods, Boe and others (2010) found that 2066–2085 is the first 20-year period with climatologically ice-free conditions throughout the Arctic in September.

In contrast to the hemispheric studies described above that focused on September, this study was both regional and year-round in scope. Wang and Overland's (2009) two-stage approach for defining GCM subsets was used here to ensure that a seasonality constraint was imposed on the specific regions of interest. However, the exact metrics and criteria used by Wang and Overland in their hemispheric study were modified for this analysis of the Bering and Chukchi Seas for two reasons. First, because the Bering Sea is completely ice-free during summer, and the Chukchi Sea completely ice-covered in winter, neither study area benefited by measuring seasonality as the difference between the annual maximum and minimum ice extent, because one endpoint remained constant in all years. Instead, the annual number of observed ice-free months was used to assess whether a given GCM reasonably emulated the seasonal cycle.

Second, variance thresholds were used to screen the GCMs rather than a constant tolerance of the observed mean (for example, ±20 percent). Using thresholds that reflected a region's observed variance accommodated the highly variable summer ice conditions in the Chukchi Sea without being too restrictive, as well as the relatively constant winter conditions in the Bering Sea without being too liberal. However, even 1 standard deviation of the observed mean ice-free months in the Chukchi Sea included zero because ice-free conditions there have been rare until only recently. Hence, to impart a non-zero lower bound for the Chukchi Sea, selected GCMs also were required to simulate at least 1 ice-free month during 1979–2008. The rationale was to exclude GCMs that showed no intrinsic capacity to generate an ice-free month in the Chukchi Sea during the observational period. Models simulating an unreasonably high number of ice-free months, however, were still excluded by the upper bound of the observed variance.

Model subsetting or weighting is a commonly applied approach to reduce the broad spread of uncertainty that exists among the full suite of CMIP3 sea ice projections. Positive correlations between sea ice hindcasts and projections provide evidence that at least some models possess an inherent degree of bias. In other words, models that simulate thicker or more extensive ice typically are models that retain more ice in their future projections, and models that simulate thinner or less extensive ice retain less ice in their future projections (Boe and others, 2010; Holland and others, 2010). Boe and others (2010) capitalize on this correlation to constrain the high degree of uncertainty that exists among the full suite of CMIP3 ice projections.

Ideally, the uncertainties within and among different GCM model runs would simply reflect differences stemming from the Earth's natural climate variability. But GCM uncertainties also are comprised of 'errors' that commonly are attributed to the various ways in which different models infer the dynamical effects of various physical processes that occur at spatial scales finer than the GCM grid itself (Randall and others, 2007). This procedure is termed sub-grid scale parameterization. Uncertainties associated with a metric like global mean annual temperature (GMAT) may be dominated by the effects of sub-grid scale parameterization because GMAT expresses such a comprehensive integration of the entire model. However, sea ice is but one component of a GCM, and while not immune to the influences of sub-grid parameterizations, other sources can act to inflate the spread of uncertainty. One notable source rests in the different degrees of sophistication among the sea ice models (Zhang and Walsh, 2006). CCSM3 and HadGEM1 are recognized as relatively sophisticated models that generally simulate observations better than others (Gerdes and Köberle, 2007). In contrast, some models lack an up-to-date physical treatment of sea ice dynamics that make them candidates for lesser weighting or exclusion (Zhang, 2010). In this study, another source of uncertainty may have been introduced by using global models to examine regional sea ice, and in so doing, capturing a model's local-scale bias that may have had little net effect on its global performance.

Screening GCMs begs an irresolvable question regarding how many models should be retained or excluded (Tebaldi and Knutti, 2007). The desire is to remove models that so extremely misrepresent observations that the models can be suspected of producing unreliable projections, while at the same time retaining a large enough number of models to robustly represent the uncertainties associated with natural climate variability and sub-grid scale parameterizations. DeWeaver (2007) and Stroeve and others (2007) required models to simulate ice cover to within ±20 percent of the observed mean because the threshold imposed a reasonable constraint while retaining a sufficient sample size to argue that the ensemble's range of uncertainty had not be unduly compromised. The SD2 subsets of this study retained 10–11 models (table 1), similar to the number of models retained by the aforementioned studies.

Although the more restrictive SD1 model subset for the Bering Sea consistently reduced the spread of uncertainty compared to its SD2 counterpart, the reduction was less apparent for the Chukchi Sea SD1 subset (figs. 4, 5, 8, 11, and 12). Favoring the less restrictive and hence larger SD2 subset over the SD1 subset may be preferable to assuming that an ensemble with as few as four models (table 1) includes a defensible range of representative uncertainty.

A multi-model median projection can be viewed as a collective 'best guess' by the models comprising the ensemble. Interpreting a median projection alone essentially dismisses consideration of the ensemble's uncertainty. Nevertheless, a 'best guess' is a practical starting point to benchmark anticipated changes and establish a framework from which to assess ecological implications or adaptive capacities. Uncertainties can be assessed thereafter. Large uncertainties may prove intractable for some topics or questions, but the spread of uncertainty may be inconsequential for others.

Ice-free conditions in the Chukchi Sea are attained for a 3-month period (August–October) at the end of the century (fig. 7) with almost complete agreement among models of the SD2 subset (fig. 12). Consequently, a higher degree of confidence can accompany hypotheses or decisions premised on this outcome and timeframe. Greater confidence also accompanies the projection that the Chukchi Sea will be completely ice covered at the end of the century during February–April (fig. 8). However, large uncertainties are prevalent during the intervening melt and freeze seasons; most notably in June, November, and December. Part of this large uncertainty might stem from larger natural variability associated with a vast area like the Chukchi Sea cycling between an ice-covered and ice-free state. Satellite observations of the Chukchi Sea provide empirical evidence that higher variability accompanies higher fluxes in ice cover; especially during the months of peak melt and freeze (fig. 3). Because the entire Arctic is projected to oscillate between an ice-free and ice-covered state before the end of the century (Boe and others, 2010), interannual variability in the timing and extent of partial ice cover in the Chukchi Sea might be expected to increase in the coming decades (Goosse and others, 2009).

Stroeve and others (2007) revealed that none or very few of the individual CMIP3 GCM simulations showed declining sea ice trends that were comparable to observations. Since Stroeve's publication, minimum ice extents for the summers of 2007, 2008, and 2009 have been well below the previous 2005 record, further substantiating that the observed rate of sea ice decline is progressing 'faster than forecasted'. After intermittently losing unusually large amounts of multiyear sea ice during the past 2 decades (Rigor and others, 2002; Nghiem and others, 2007; Zhang and others, 2008; Ogi and others, 2010), the Arctic's pack ice is now thinner (Yu and others, 2004; Kwok and others, 2009), younger (Rigor and Wallace, 2004; Belchansky and others, 2005; Maslanik and others, 2007), and more vulnerable to longer summer melt seasons (Belchansky and others, 2004; Markus and others, 2009) and positive feedbacks (Perovich and others, 2007). The present condition of Arctic sea ice and its steep rate of decline warrant serious consideration to the possibility that the CMIP3 GCM projections collectively portray 21st century sea ice losses on a conservative time frame.

As a new generation of GCM projections are prepared for the IPCC's fifth assessment, it should be recognized that a high degree of uncertainty among models will likely persist. Some models will be improved by attaining higher spatial resolution, but the uncertainties of sub-grid scale parameterization will not be resolved. Some models will strive to elaborate dynamics of the carbon cycle and terrestrial landcover change that will, in turn, introduce new sources of uncertainty. In practice, and by construct, GMCs will continue to possess uncertainty. Nevertheless, GCMs provide a state-of-the-art and practical starting point to benchmark anticipated changes and establish a framework from which to assess ecological implications or adaptive capacities, including assessments of both the benefits and costs associated with taking or not taking measures to constrain future greenhouse gas emissions.

11

Conclusions

This report presents a detailed examination of future sea ice conditions in the Bering and Chukchi Seas based on projections by 18 GCMs from the CMIP3 multi-model dataset. All GCMs project reductions in ice cover during the 21st century when forced with either of two unmitigated greenhouse gas emission scenarios (A1B and A2), but the magnitude of change varies widely among the full ensemble of models. The spread of projected uncertainty is substantially reduced among models that more reasonably simulate the past 30 years of sea ice observations. However, regardless of the emission scenario or ensemble of models, multi-model median ice projections are remarkably similar at mid-century, and even more so at the end of the century.

There is high agreement among models that the shelf waters of the Chukchi Sea will be ice-free for at least 3 months (August–October) by mid-century. By the end of the century, and with somewhat less agreement among models, the Chukchi Sea shelf could be ice free (or nearly ice free) for as many as 4–5 months. Projections of sea ice loss in June are relatively modest, so extensive areas of ice are projected to rapidly melt in July in order to achieve an ice-free state by August. There is a large spread of uncertainty with respect to the chronology of autumn freeze in the Chukchi Sea, but all models concur that the Chukchi Sea will continue to be entirely ice-covered during February, March, and April throughout the 21st century.

June is projected to be persistently ice free in the Bering Sea by mid-century, at which time most models project that May will begin to intermittently experience ice-free years. By the end of the century, delayed freeze in the Chukchi Sea lengthens the ice-free season in the Bering Sea by about 3 months overall—a 1-month advance in melt and a 2-month delay in freeze. Presently, the ice edge retreats and advances through the Bering Strait in June and November, but by the end of the century, these transition months are projected to shift to May and January. Maximum ice extent in the Bering Sea continues to be attained in March but the projected magnitude of cover varies substantially between individual models. Multi-model median projections among all ensembles, however, consistently project about a 25-percent reduction in March ice extent by mid-century and a 60-percent reduction by the end of the century, compared to the earliest decade of satellite observations (1979–1988).

Assuming robustness in the unmitigated GHG emission scenarios that were used to force the models, and robustness in the CMIP3 models themselves, there is a high degree of certainty that by the end of the century, the Chukchi Sea will be ice free for several months during the summer, and that the ice-free season in Bering Sea will be extended by several months. The breadth of uncertainty among the model projections essentially rests in their subtle but different outcomes of precisely how many months will be ice free, which in turn affects their rates of projected change during the melt and freeze seasons.

Acknowledgments

This study was funded by the U.S. Geological Survey (USGS) to provide science support to the U.S. Fish and Wildlife Service, and to address science objectives underlying the USGS Alaska Science Center's research on global climate change and changing Arctic ecosystems. Suggestions and critiques by J. Overland, M. Wang, and E. DeWeaver greatly improved the scope and content of this report. The modeling groups, the Program for Climate Model Diagnosis and Intercomparison, and the World Climate Research Program's Working Group on Coupled Modelling are acknowledged for their roles in making available the CMIP3 multi-model dataset. Support of the CMIP3 dataset is provided by the Office of Science, U.S. Department of Energy.

References Cited

Arctic Climate Impact Assessment, 2005, Arctic Climate Impact Assessment: New York, Cambridge University Press, 1042 p., accessed August 5, 2010, at *http://www.acia.uaf.edu*.

Alexander, V., and Niebauer, H.J., 1981, Oceanography of the eastern Bering Sea ice-edge zone in spring: Limnology and Oceanography, v. 26, no. 6, p. 1111–1125.

Barry, R.G., Serreze, M.C., and Maslanik, J.A., 1993, The Arctic sea ice-climate system—Observations and modeling: Reviews of Geophysics, v. 31, no. 4, p. 397–422.

Boe, J., Hall, A. and Qu, X., 2010, September sea-ice cover in the Arctic Ocean projected to vanish by 2100: Nature Geoscience, v. 2, p. 341–343 (also available at *http://dx.doi.org/10.1038/NGEO467*).

Belchansky, G.I., Douglas, D.C., and Platonov, N.G., 2004, Duration of the Arctic sea ice melt season—Regional and interannual variability, 1979–2001: Journal of Climate, v. 17, p. 67–80.

Belchansky, G.I., Douglas, D.C., and Platonov, N.G., 2005, Spatial and temporal variations in the age structure of Arctic sea ice: Geophysical Research Letters. v. 32, p. L18504 (also available at *http://dx.doi.org/10.1029/2005GL023976*.

Bering Ecosystem Study, 2004, Bering Ecosystem Study (BEST) Science Plan: Fairbanks, Alaska, Arctic Research Consortium of the U.S., 82 p.

Budikova, D., 2009, Role of Arctic sea ice in global atmospheric circulation: A review. Global Planetary Change, v. 68, p. 149–163.

Cavalieri, D., Parkinson, C., Gloersen, P., and Zwally, H.J., 1996 [updated 2008], Sea ice concentrations from Nimbus-7 SMMR and DMSP SSM/I passive microwave data, 1979–2007: Boulder, Colo., National Snow and Ice Data Center [Digital media].

Cavalieri, D.J., Parkinson, C.L., Gloersen, P., Comiso, J.C., and Zwally, H.J., 1999, Deriving long-term time series of sea ice cover from satellite passive-microwave multisensor data sets: Journal of Geophysical Research, v. 104, p. 15803–15814.

Comiso, J.C., Yang, J., Honjo, S., and Krishfield, R.A., 2003, Detection and change in the Arctic using satellite and in situ data: Journal of Geophysical Research, v. 108, p. 3384 (also available at *http://dx.doi.org/10.1029/2002JC001347*).

Comiso, J.C., Parkinson, C.L., Gersten, R., and Stock, L., 2008, Accelerated decline in the Arctic sea ice cover: Geophysical Research Letters, v. 35, p. L01703 (also available at *http://dx.doi.org/10.1029/2007GL031972*).

DeWeaver, E., 2007, Uncertainty in climate model projections of Arctic sea ice decline—An evaluation relevant to polar bears: U.S. Geological Survey Administrative Report, 47 p. (Also available at *http://www.usgs.gov/newsroom/special/polar_bears/*)

Fay, F.H., 1985, *Odobenus rosmarus*: Mammalian Species, no. 238, 7 p.

Gerdes, R., and Köberle, C., 2007, Comparison of Arctic sea ice thickness variability in IPCC climate models of the 20th century experiments and in ocean-sea ice hindcasts: Journal of Geophysical Research, v. 112, p. C04S13 (also available at *http://dx.doi.org/10.1029/2006JC003616*).

Gleckler, P.J., Taylor, K.E., and Doutriaux, C., 2008, Performance metrics for climate models: Journal of Geophysical Research, v. 113, p. D06104 (also available at *http://dx.doi.org/10.1029/2007JD008972*).

Goosse, H., Arzel, O., Bitz, C.M., de Montety, A., and Vancoppenolle, M., 2009, Increased variability of the Arctic summer ice extent in a warmer climate: Geophysical Research Letters, v. 36, p. L23702, (also available at *http://dx.doi.org/10.1029/2009GL040546*).

Grebmeier, J.M., Overland, J.E., Moore, S.E., Farley, E.V., Carmack, E.C., Cooper, L.W., Frey, K.E., Helle, J.H., McLaughlin, F.A., and McNutt, S.L., 2006, A major ecosystem shift in the northern Bering Sea: Science, v. 311, no. 5766, p. 1461–1464 (also available at *http://dx.doi.org/10.1126/science.1121365*).

Grebmeier, J.M., Moore, S.E., Overland, J.E., Frey, K.E., and Gradinger, R., 2010, Biological response to recent Pacific arctic sea ice retreats: EOS Transactions, v. 91, no. 18, p. 161–162.

Hawkins, E., and Sutton, R., 2009, The potential to narrow uncertainty in regional climate predictions: Bulletin of the American Meteorological Society, v. 90, p. 1095–1107 (also available at *http://dx.doi.org/10.1175/2009BAMS2607.1*).

Holland, M.M., Bitz, C.M., and Tremblay, B., 2006, Future abrupt reductions in the summer Arctic sea ice. Geophysical Research Letters, v. 33, p. L23503 (also available at *http://dx.doi.org/10.1029/2006GL028024*).

Holland, M.M., Bailey, D.A., and Vavrus, S., 2010, Inherent sea ice predictability in the rapidly changing Arctic environment of the Community Climate System Model, version 3: Climate Dynamics (also available at *http://dx.doi.org/10.1007/s00382-010-0792-4*).

Hovelsrud, G.K., McKenna, M., and Huntington, H.P., 2008, Marine mammal harvests and other interactions with humans: Ecological Applications, v. 18, no. 2 (Supplement), p. S135–S147.

Intergovernmental Panel on Climate Change, 2007, Summary for Policy Makers, *in* Solomon, S., Qin, D., Manning, M., and Miller, H.L. (eds.), Climate Change, The Physical Science Basis: Contribution of Working Group I to the Fourth Assessment Report of the Intergovernmental Panel on Climate Change: New York and Oxford, Cambridge University Press.

Johannessen, O.M., Bengtsson, L., Miles, M.W., Kuzmina, S., Semenov, V.A., Alekseev, G.V., Naurnyi, A.P., Zakharov, V., Bobylev, L.P., Pettersson, L.H., Hasselmann, K., and Cattle, H.P., 2004, Arctic climate change—Observed and modelled temperature and sea ice: Tellus, v. 56A, p. 328–341.

Knutti, R., 2008, Should we believe model predictions of future climate change? Philosophical Transactions of the Royal Society A, v. 366, p. 4647–4664 (also available at *http://dx.doi.org/10.1098/rsta.2008.0169*).

Kwok, R., Cunningham, G.F., Wensnahan, M., Rigor, I., Zwally, H.J., and Yi, D., (2009), Thinning and volume loss of the Arctic Ocean sea ice cover: 2003–2008: Journal of Geophysical Research, v. 114, C07005 (also available at *http://dx.doi.org/10.1029/2009JC005312*).

Minerals Management Service, 2008, Outer continental shelf (OCS) Chukchi Sea Alaska, oil and gas lease sale 193: Federal Register, v. 73, no. 1, 209–213.

Markus, T., Stroeve, J.C., and Miller, J., 2009, Recent changes in Arctic sea ice melt onset, freezeup, and melt season length: Journal of Geophysical Research, v. 114, p. C12024 (also available at *http://dx.doi.org/10.1029/2009JC005436*).

Maslanik, J.A., Fowler, C., Stroeve, J., Drobot, S., Zwally, J., Yi, D., and Emery, W., 2007, A younger, thinner Arctic ice cover: Increased potential for rapid, extensive sea-ice loss: Geophysical Research Letters, v. 34, p. L24501 (also available at *http://dx.doi.org/10.1029/2007GL032043*).

McGuffie, K., and Henderson-Sellers, A., 2005, A Climate Modelling Primer (3d ed.): London, John Wiley and Sons, Ltd., 280 p.

Meehl, G.A., Covey, C., Delworth, T., Latif, M., McAvaney, B., Mitchell, J.F.B., Stouffer, R.J., and Taylor, K.E., 2007a, The WCRP CMIP3 multi model dataset—A new era in climate change research: Bulletin of the American Meteorological Society, v. 88, p. 1383–1394.

Meehl, G.A., Stocker, T.F., Collins, W.D., Friedlingstein, P., Gaye, A.T., Gregory, J.M., Kitoh, A., Knutti, R., Murphy, J.M., Noda, A., Raper, S.C.B., Watterson, I.G., Weaver A.J., and Zhao, Z.-C., 2007b, Global Climate Projections, *in* Solomon, S., Qin, D., Manning, M., Chen, Z., Marquis, M., Averyt, K.B., Tignor, M., and Miller, H.L. (eds.), 2007b, Climate Change 2007—The Physical Science Basis: Contribution of Working Group I to the Fourth Assessment Report of the Intergovernmental Panel on Climate Change: New York and Cambridge: Cambridge University Press, p. 747–845.

Meier, W.N., Stroeve, J., and Fetterer, F., 2007, Whither Arctic sea ice? A clear signal of decline regionally, seasonally and extending beyond the satellite record: Annals of Glaciology, v. 46, p. 428–434.

Meier, W., Fetterer, F., Knowles, K., Savoie, M., and Brodzik, M.J., 2006 [updated quarterly], Sea ice concentrations from Nimbus-7 SMMR and DMSP SSM/I passive microwave data, 2008: Boulder, Colo., National Snow and Ice Data Center [Digital media].

Moore, S.E., and Huntington, H.P., 2008, Arctic marine mammals and climate change—Impacts and resilience: Ecological Applications, v. 18, no. 2 (Supplement), p. S157–S165.

Nakicenovic, N., Alcama, J., Davis, G., de Vries, B., Fenhann, J., Gaffin, S., Gregory, K., and 21 others, 2000, Emissions Scenarios—A Special Report of Working Group III of the Intergovernmental Panel on Climate Change: Cambridge, Cambridge University Press.

Nordquist, M.H., Moore, J.N., and Heidar, T.H., eds., 2010, Changes in the Arctic Environment and the Law of the Sea: Brill Academic Publishers, Inc., 594 p.

Nghiem, S.V., Rigor, I.G., Perovich, D.K., Clemente-Colón, P., and Weatherly, J.W., 2007, Rapid reduction of Arctic perennial sea ice: Geophysical Research Letters, v. 34, p. L19504 (also available at *http://dx.doi.org/10.1029/2007GL031138*).

National Snow and Ice Data Center, 2010, State of the Cryosphere, accessed August 5, 2010, at *http://nsidc.org/sotc/sea_ice.html*.

Ogi, M., Yamzaki, K., and Wallace, J.M., 2010, Influence of winter and summer wind anomalies on summer Arctic sea ice extent: Geophysical Research Letters, v. 37, p. L07701 (also available at *http://dx.doi.org/10.1029/2009GL042356*).

Perovich, D.K., and Richter-Menge, J.A., 2009, Loss of sea ice in the Arctic: Annual Review of Marine Science, v. 1, p. 417–441 (also available at *http://dx.doi.org/10.1146/annurev.marine.010908.163805*).

Perovich, D.K., Light, B., Eicken, H., Jones, K.F., Runciman, K., and Nghiem, S.V., 2007, Increasing solar heating of the Arctic Ocean and adjacent seas, 1979-2005—Attribution and role of the ice-albedo feedback: Geophysical Research Letters, v. 34, p. L19505 (also available at *http://dx.doi.org/10.1029/2007GL031480*).

Randall, D.A., Wood, R.A., Bony, S., Colman, R., Fichefet, T., Fyfe, J., Kattsov, V., Pitman, A., Shukla, J., Srinivasan, J., Stouffer, R.J., Sumi A., and Taylor, K.E., 2007, Climate Models and Their Evaluation, *in* Solomon, S., Qin, D., Manning, M., Chen, Z., Marquis, M., Averyt, K.B., Tignor, M., and Miller, H.L., eds., Climate Change 2007—The Physical Science Basis. Contribution of Working Group I to the Fourth Assessment Report of the Intergovernmental Panel on Climate Change: New York and Cambridge, Cambridge University Press, p. 589–662.

Rigor, I.G., Wallace, J.M., and Colony, R.L., 2002, Response of sea ice to the Arctic Oscillation: Journal of Climate, v. 15, no. 18, p. 2648–2663.

Rigor, I.G., and Wallace, J.M., 2004, Variations in the age of Arctic sea-ice and summer sea-ice extent: Geophysical Research Letter, v. 31, p. L09401 (also available at *http://dx.doi.org/10.1029/2004GL019492*).

Serreze, M.C., Holland, M.M., and Stroeve, J., 2007, Perspectives on the Arctic's shrinking sea-ice cover: Science, v. 315, p. 1533–1536 (also available at *http://dx.doi.org/10.1126/science.1139426*).

Springer, A.M., Piatt, J.F., Shuntov, V.P., Van Vliet, G.B., Vladimirov, V.L., Kuzin, A.E., and Perlov, A.S., 1999, Marine birds and mammals of the Pacific subarctic gyres: Progress in Oceanography, v. 43, p. 443–487.

Springer, A.M., McRoy, C.P., and Flint, M.V., 1996, The Bering Sea green belt—shelf-edge processes and ecosystem production: Fisheries Oceanography, v. 5, nos. 3–4, p. 205–223.

Stroeve, J., Holland, M.M., Meier, W., Scambos, T., and Serreze, M., 2007, Arctic sea ice decline—Faster than forecast: Geophysical Research Letters, v. 34, p. L09501 (also available at *http://dx.doi.org/10.1029/2007GL029703*).

Tebaldi, C., and Knutti, R., 2007, The use of the multi-model ensemble in probabilistic climate projections: Philosophical Transactions of the Royal Society A, v. 365, p. 2053–2075 (also available at *http://dx.doi.org/10.1098/rsta.2007.2076*).

Vilhjálmsson, H., and Hoel, A.H., 2005, Fisheries and aquaculture, Chapter 13, *in* Arctic Climate Impact Assessment: New York, Cambridge University Press, 1042 p., accessed August 5, 2010, at *http://www.acia.uaf.edu*.

Wang, M., and Overland, J.E., 2009, A sea ice free summer Arctic within 30 years? Geophysical Research Letters, v. 36, p. L07502 (also available at *http://dx.doi.org/10.1029/2009GL037820*).

Woodgate, R.A., and Aagaard, K., 2005, Revising the Bering Strait freshwater flux into the Arctic Ocean: Geophysical Research Letters, v. 32, p. L02602 (also available at *http://dx.doi.org/10.1029/2004GL021747*).

Woodgate, R.A., Weingartner, T., and Lindsay, R., 2010, The 2007 Bering Strait oceanic heat flux and anomalous Arctic sea-ice retreat: Geophysical Research Letters, v. 37, p. L01602 (also available at *http://dx.doi.org/10.1029/2009GL041621*).

Yu, Y., Maykut, G.A., and Rothrock, D.A., 2004, Changes in the thickness distribution of Arctic sea ice between 1958–1970 and 1993–1997: Journal of Geophysical Research, v. 109, p. c08004 (also available at *http://dx.doi.org/10.1029/2003JC001982*).

Zhang, J., Lindsay, R., Steele, M., and Schweiger, A., 2008, What drove the dramatic retreat of arctic sea ice during the summer of 2007? Geophysical Research Letters, v. 35, p. L11505 (also available at *http://dx.doi.org/10.1029/2008GL034005*).

Zhang, X., 2010, Sensitivity of arctic summer sea ice coverage to global warming forcing: towards reducing uncertainty in arctic climate change projections: Tellus, v. 62A, p. 220–227 (also available at *http://dx.doi.org/10.1111/j.1600-0870.2010.00441.x*).

Zhang, X., and Walsh, J.E., 2006, Toward a seasonally ice-covered Arctic Ocean—Scenarios from the IPCC AR4 model simulations: Journal of Climate, v. 19, p. 1730–1747.

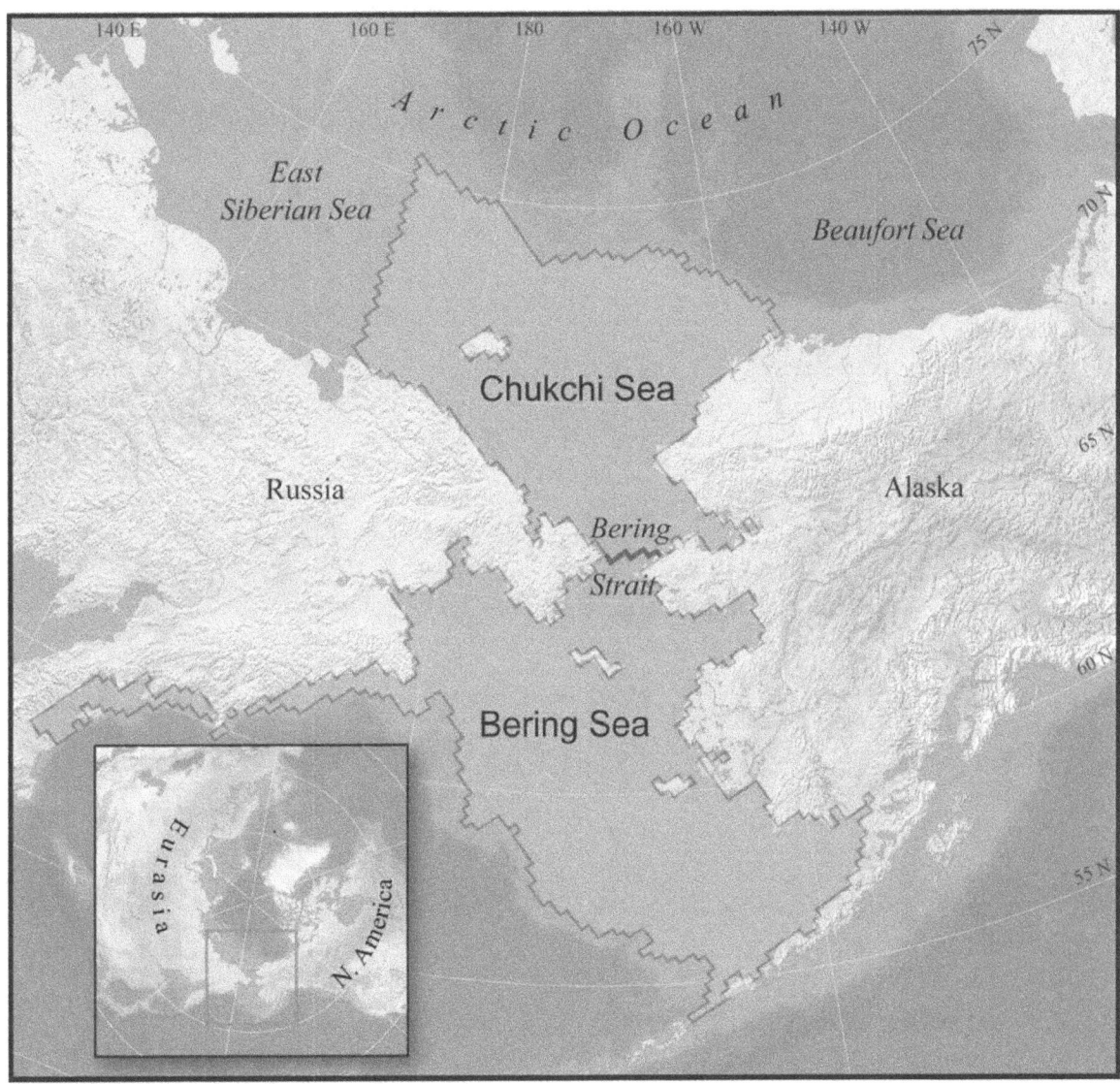

Figure 1. Extent of the Chukchi Sea and Bering Sea study areas (green shade), spanning shelf waters greater than −150 meters deep and bounded longitudinally by the distribution of the Pacific walrus population. The two study areas are divided by the Bering Strait. The Chukchi and Bering Seas are located between North America and Eurasia (inset).

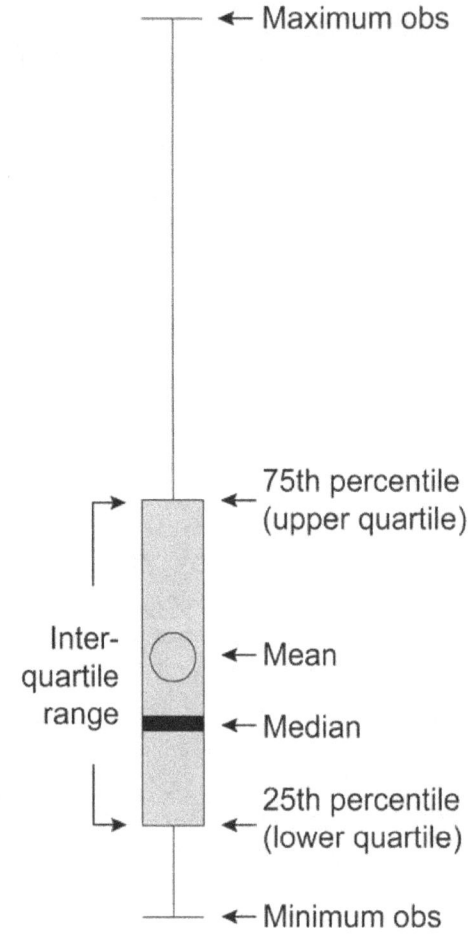

Figure 2. Box and whisker notation used in this report.

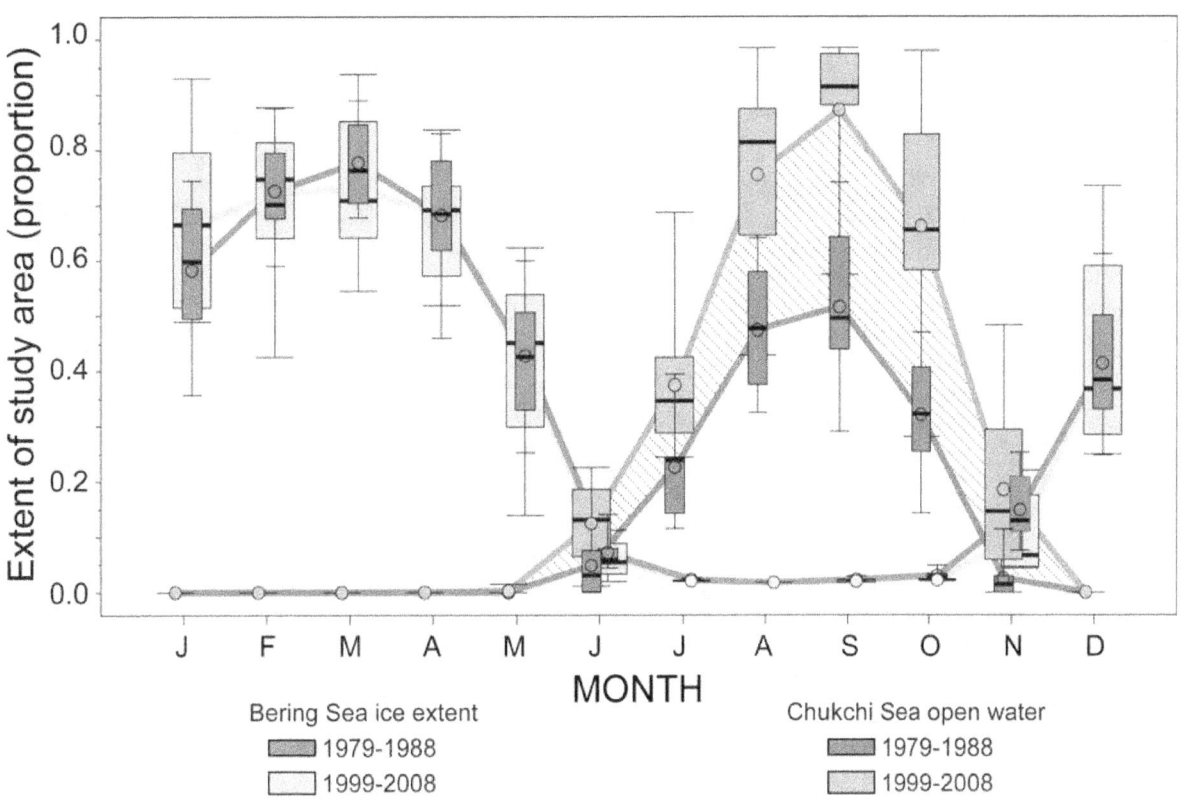

Figure 3. Monthly proportional extent of ice in the Bering Sea and open water in the Chukchi Sea, during the earliest and most recent decades of the satellite data record. Hatched area highlights the recent decline of summer ice in the Chukchi Sea in contrast to the relatively constant extent of winter ice in the Bering Sea. Box-and-whisker plots are constructed from the 10 years of observations within a respective decade.

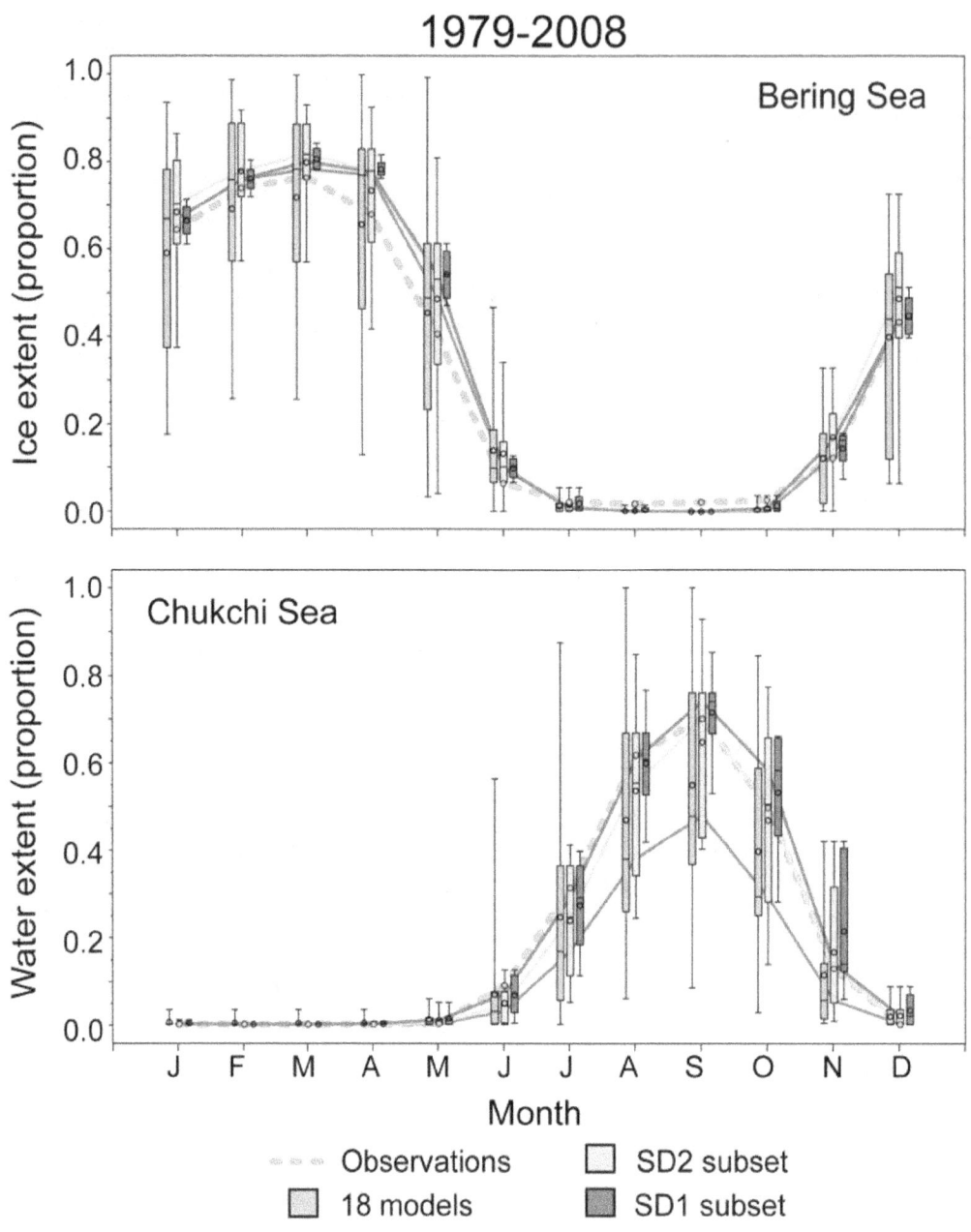

Figure 4. Monthly proportional ice extent in the Bering Sea and open water in the Chukchi Sea, simulated by 18 GCMs and 2 GCM subsets, and as observed by satellite during 1979–2008. GCM simulations for the late 20th century used the 20C3M forcing scenario and A1B forcing scenario for the early years of the 21st century. Box-and-whisker plots are constructed from the 30-year averages of each model in the respective model ensemble (table 1). Lines join observed means and multi-model medians. Box and whiskers are slightly offset left and right of the monthly tics for legibility.

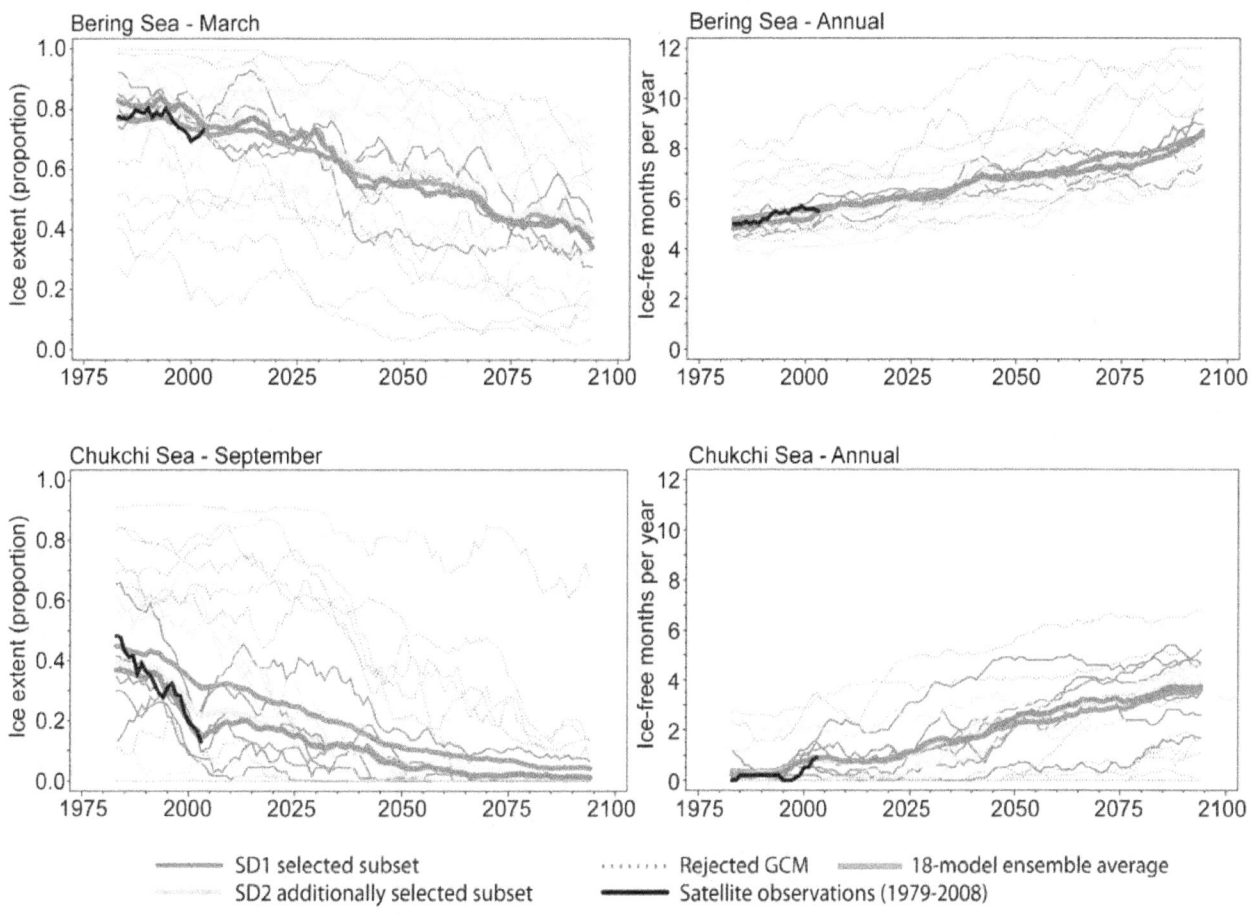

Figure 5. Late 20th century simulations and 21st century projections of March ice cover and total annual ice-free months in the Bering Sea, and September ice cover and total annual ice-free months in the Chukchi Sea, by 18 GCMs and 2 selected GCM subsets with the A1B forced scenario. GCMs from the SD1 subset are plotted with red lines, and the additional GCMs that comprise the SD2 subset are plotted with yellow lines (that is, SD2 = red and yellow lines). Rejected GCMs are plotted with gray dotted lines. Multi-model averages are plotted as bold lines, and the average of all 18 models as a bold gray line. Satellite observations are black lines. All lines depict 10-year centered moving averages.

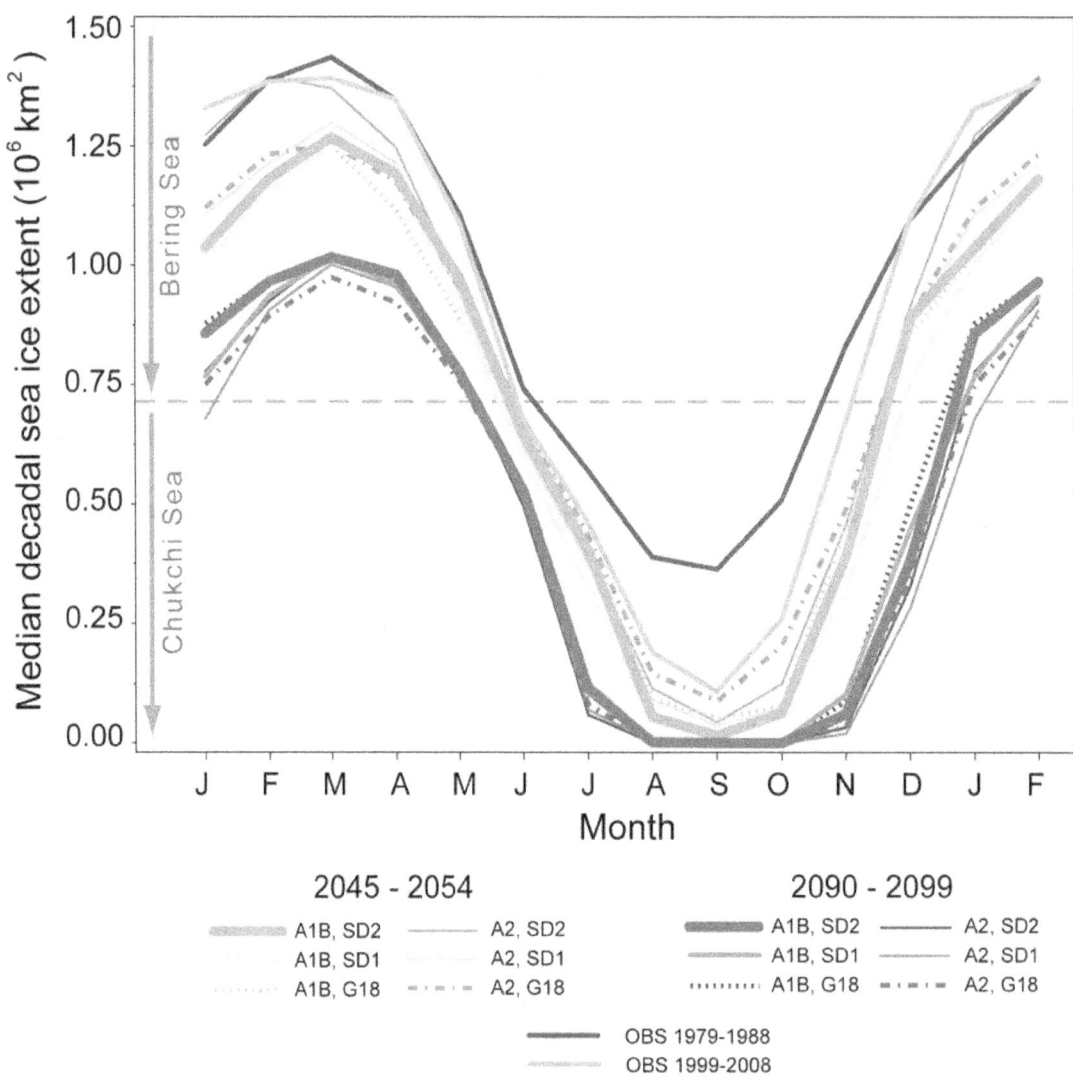

Figure 6. Projected sea ice extent in the combined Bering and Chukchi Seas during the mid- and late 21st century by 18 CMIP3 general circulation models (G18), and 2 selected model subsets (SD2 and SD1). Projections are shown for each of two greenhouse gas forcing scenarios (A1B and A2). Plotted are monthly multi-model medians derived from the average decadal ice extents of the respective ensemble models. Horizontal dotted line approximates the Bering Strait transition zone. Observed ice extents during early and recent decades of satellite observations are shown to benchmark recent and projected change. January and February are repeated on the x-axis to add visual continuity to the full annual cycle.

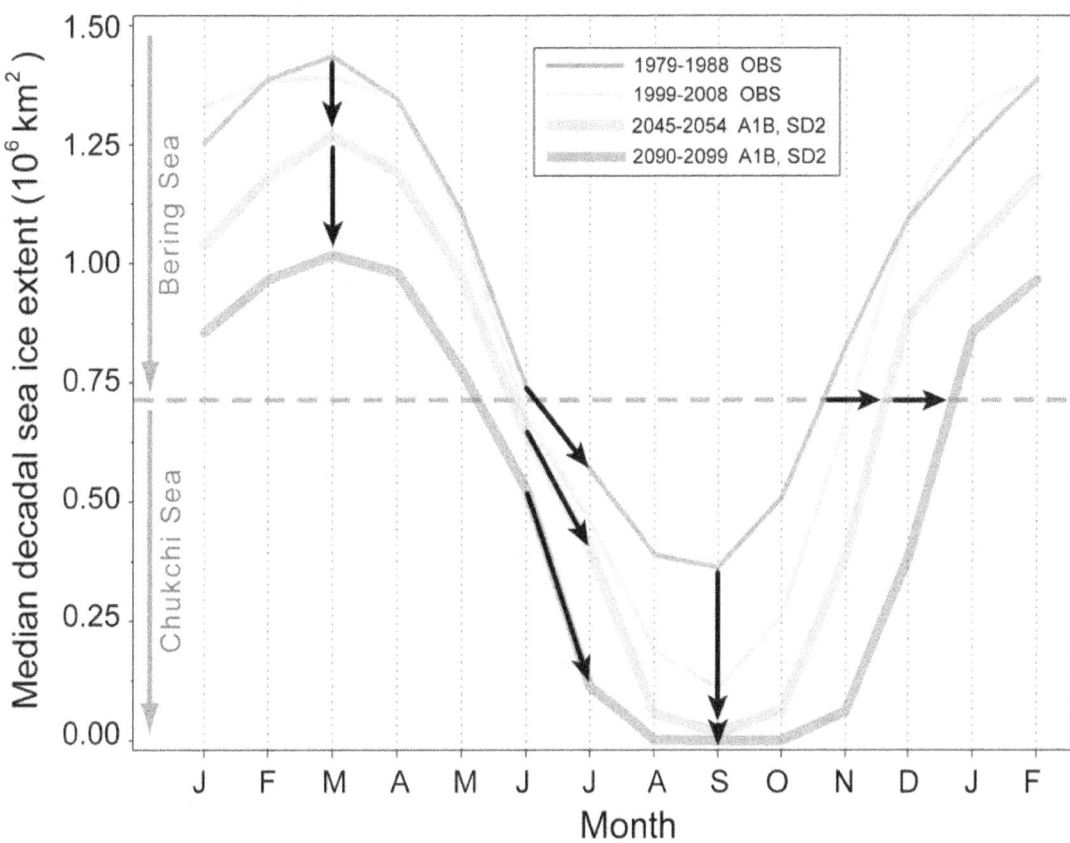

Figure 7. General patterns of projected sea ice changes in the combined Bering and Chukchi Seas (adapted from figure 6). Vertical arrows highlight magnitudes of projected declines in ice extent between the early decade of observations to mid-century, and mid- to late-century. Inclined arrows highlight projected increases in the area of early summer ice melt, and horizontal arrows highlight projected delays in complete freeze of the Chukchi Sea. Horizontal dotted line approximates the Bering Strait transition zone.

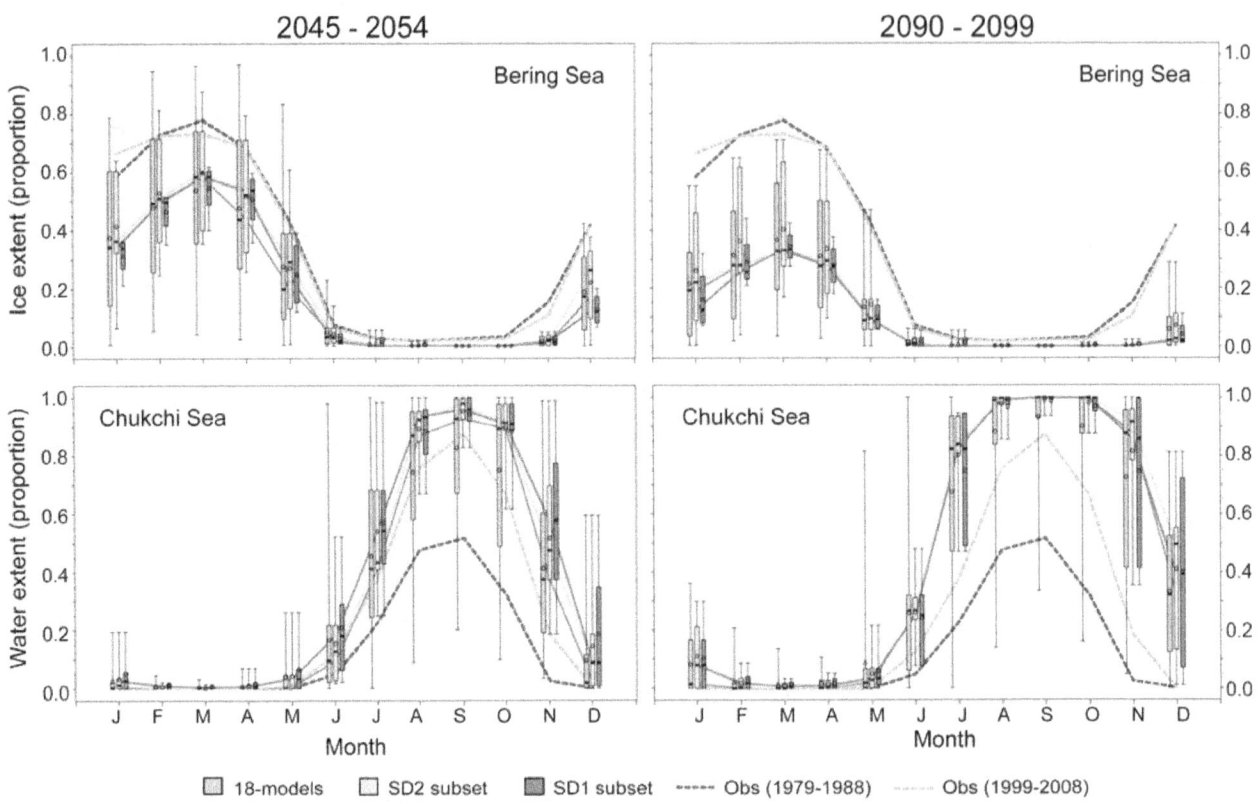

Figure 8. Projected monthly proportional ice extent in the Bering Sea, and open water in the Chukchi Sea during the mid- and last decades of the 21st century by 18 GCMs and 2 selected GCM subsets with the A1B forced scenario. Two decades of satellite observations are shown to benchmark recent and projected change. Box-and-whisker plots were constructed from the decadal averages of each model in the respective ensemble. Lines join observed means and multi-model medians. Box and whiskers are slightly offset left and right of the monthly tics for legibility.

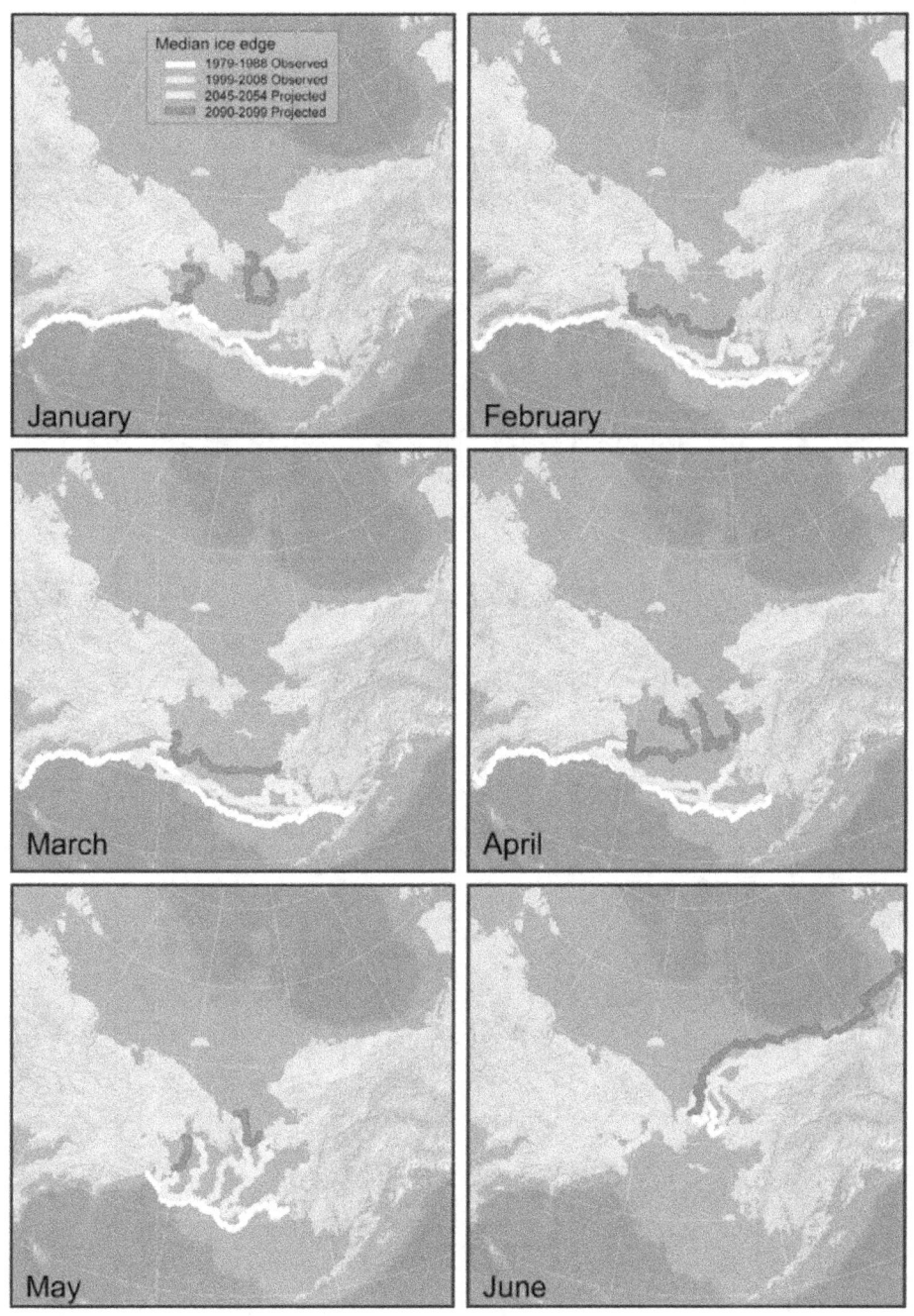

Figure 9. Monthly location of projected median sea ice edges at mid- (yellow) and late (red) century based on A1B forcing scenario and the Bering Sea SD2 subset in December–May and the Chukchi Sea SD2 subset in June–November. The observed median ice edge for 1979–1988 (white) and 1999–2008 (green) are shown to benchmark recent and projected change. Median ice edges demarcate where greater than 50 percent of the years (for observations) or models × years (for projections) were covered by ice with greater than15 percent concentration.

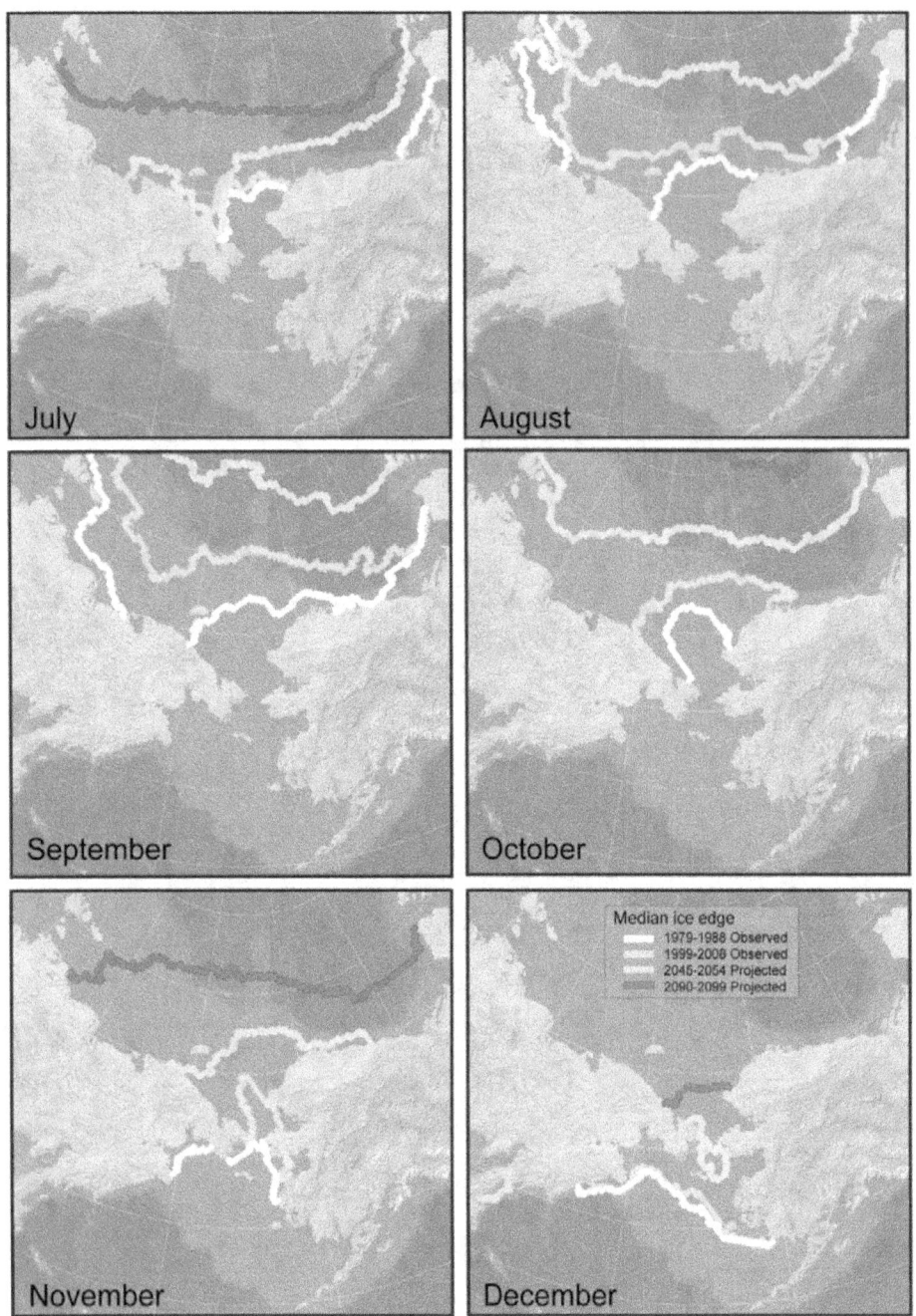

Figure 9.— Continued.

The projected median ice edge during August and September of 2090–2099 occurs north of this map extent.

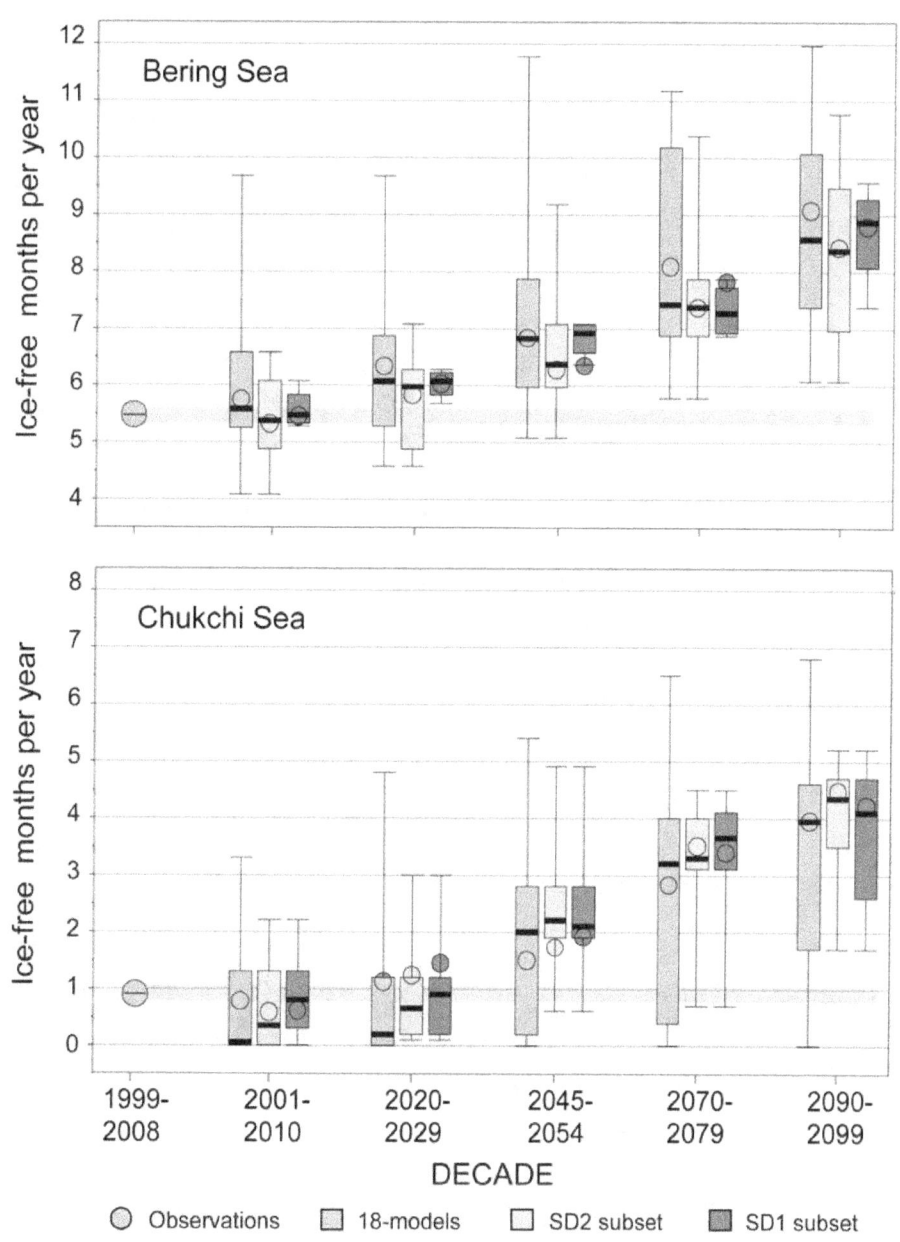

Figure 10. Number of ice-free months per year for 5 decadal periods spanning the 21st century, projected by 18 GCMs and 2 selected GCM subsets (SD2 and SD1). GCM projections are based on the A1B forced scenario. The most recent decadal average from satellite observations is shown to benchmark projected changes (blue dot with extended reference line). Box-and-whisker plots were constructed from the decadal averages of each model in the respective ensemble.

27

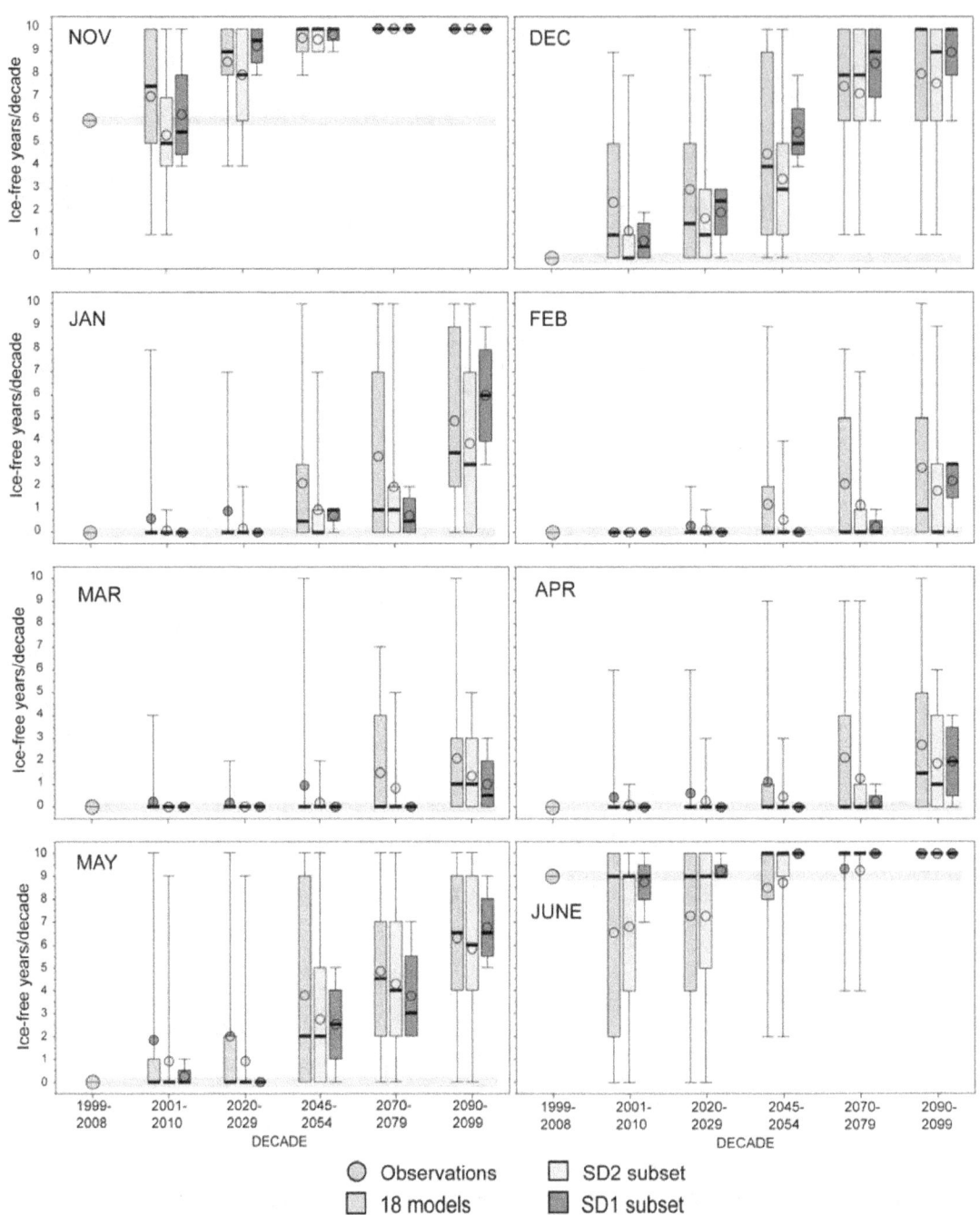

Figure 11. Number of years per decade projected to be ice-free in the Bering Sea by 18 GCMs and 2 selected GCM subsets (SD2 and SD1), for each month, during each of 5 decadal periods spanning the 21st century. GCM projections are based on the A1B forced scenario. The recent decade of satellite observations (blue dot and extended reference line) is shown to benchmark projected change. Box-and-whisker plots are constructed from the total number of ice free years (max = 10) projected by each model in the ensemble for the respective month and decade. July–October were predominantly ice-free and not shown.

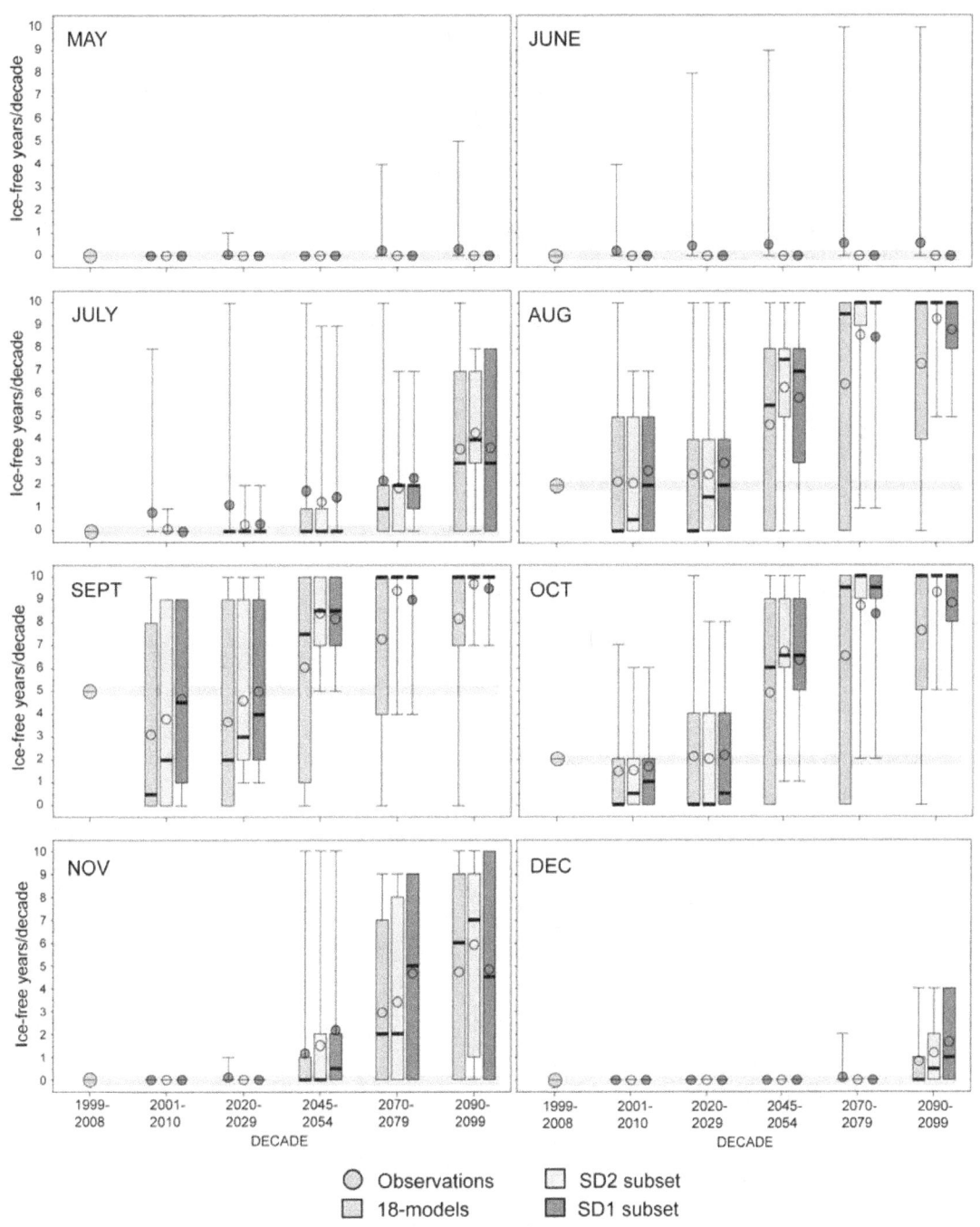

Figure 12. Number of years per decade projected to be ice-free in the Chukchi Sea by 18 GCMs and 2 selected GCM subsets (SD2 and SD1), for each month, during each of 5 decadal periods spanning the 21st century. GCM projections are based on the A1B scenario. The recent decade of satellite observations (blue dot and extended reference line) is shown to benchmark projected change. Box-and-whisker plots are constructed from the total number of ice-free years (max = 10) projected by each model in the ensemble for the respective month and decade. January–April were predominantly ice-covered and not shown.

Table 1. General circulation models used in this study and their status in each of two model subsets for the Bering Sea and Chukchi Sea study areas.

[Models were selected when both their mean ice extent and seasonality during 1979–2008 were respectively within 2 standard deviations (SD2) and 1 standard deviation (SD1) of the observed means. For the Chukchi Sea, GCMs included in a subset also were required to simulate at least 1 ice-free month during the 30-year period]

Country	CMIP3 GCM ID	Bering Sea		Chukchi Sea	
		SD2	SD1	SD2	SD1
Norway	BCCR-BCM2.0				
USA	CCSM3	X	X	X	
Canada	CGCM3.1(T47)				
France	CNRM-CM3	X		X	
Australia	CSIRO-Mk3.0				
Australia	CSIRO-Mk3.5			X	X
Germany	ECHAM5/MPI-OM	X			
Germany	ECHO-G			X	X
USA	GFDL-CM2.1	X	X	X	
USA	GFDL-CM2.0	X		X	X
USA	GISS-ER	X	X		
Italy	INGV-SXG	X			
Russia	INM-CM3.0	X			
France	IPSL-CM4			X	X
Japan	MIROC3.2(medres)	X	X	X	
Japan	MRI-CGCM2.3.2	X			
UK	UKMO-HadCM3	X		X	X
UK	UKMO-HadGEM1			X	X
	TOTAL	11	4	10	6

Table 2. Percentage of change in the monthly proportion of sea ice extent in the Bering Sea and Chukchi Sea study areas between the earliest decade of satellite observations (1979–1988) and two future decades (2045–2054 and 2090–2099), and similarly for the most recent decade of observations (1999–2008).

[Sea ice projections are based on medians of monthly decadal averages for each GCM in the SD2 subset using the A1B forced scenario]

OBSERVED DECADE	1979–1988		1999–2008	
PROJECTED DECADE	2045–2054	2090–2099	2045–2054	2090–2099
BERING SEA				
JAN	-38 %	-62 %	-46 %	-67 %
FEB	-30 %	-62 %	-30 %	-61 %
MAR	-23 %	-58 %	-18 %	-55 %
APR	-24 %	-57 %	-24 %	-57 %
MAY	-32 %	-78 %	-29 %	-77 %
JUNE	-63 %	-88 %	-55 %	-86 %
JULY				
AUG				
SEPT				
OCT				
NOV	-88 %	-100 %	-83 %	-100 %
DEC	-37 %	-94 %	-38 %	-94 %
CHUKCHI SEA				
JAN	-1 %	-8 %	-1 %	-8 %
FEB	0 %	0 %	0 %	0 %
MAR	0 %	0 %	0 %	0 %
APR	0 %	0 %	0 %	0 %
MAY	-1 %	-3 %	-1 %	-3 %
JUNE	-8 %	-23 %	0 %	-16 %
JULY	-27 %	-79 %	-9 %	-74 %
AUG	-85 %	-99 %	-69 %	-99 %
SEPT	-95 %	-100 %	-83 %	-100 %
OCT	-87 %	-100 %	-74 %	-100 %
NOV	-46 %	-91 %	-35 %	-90 %
DEC	-9 %	-49 %	-9 %	-49 %

31